National Unification and Economic Development in Vietnam

Melanie Beresford

Lecturer in History,
University of Wollongong, Australia

St. Martin's Press
New York

All rights reserved. For information, write:
Scholarly and Reference Division,
St. Martin's Press, Inc., 175 Fifth Avenue, New York, NY 10010

First published in the United States of America in 1989

Printed in Hong Kong

ISBN 0–312–03093–2

Library of Congress Cataloging-in-Publication Data
Beresford, Melanie
National unification and economic development in Vietnam/Melanie
Beresford.
    p.   cm.
Bibliography: p.
Includes index.
ISBN 0–312–03093–2
1. Vietnam—Economic conditions.   2. Vietnam—Economic policy.
3. Nationalism—Vietnam.   4. Vietnam—Politics and government—1975–
I. Title
HC444.B47   1989
330.9597′04—dc20   89–31761
                                                             CIP

Contents

List of Tables

List of Figures

Preface

In the forty years since the end of World War II, Vietnam has been the focal point of the struggle for and against colonialism, of the war between capitalism and socialism and, more recently, of the clash between contending socialisms. For this reason, it is a much-studied area of the globe, but most Western observers have looked at Vietnam's international relations or its political and military history: the economy has been a relatively neglected area. Yet in the decade since the end of the Vietnam War it is, above all, the domestic developments which deserve attention. For the first time, a nation divided in two by the ideological schisms of the cold war has been re-unified. With a population of 65 million it has become the twelfth largest country in the world and is the third largest socialist country. It has mineral, agricultural and labour resources which could ultimately see it become a major economic power in South-East Asia. However, it remains one of the poorest economies in the world at present and the re-unification process has created difficult problems for the economic development strategy being pursued. In focusing on the theme of economic unification in this book, I hope to throw some new light on these domestic developments and on Vietnam's potential for growth in the future.

Much of the material collected during two visits to Vietnam, in December 1979 and in October–November 1985, has been used for this book. I would like to thank the many officials and cadres who gave their time to assist my research, particularly Nguyen Thi Binh who travelled with me during the latter trip and was of enormous help in the organisational sphere.

Most of the documentary research was carried out in the French National Archives, Dépôt d'Outre-Mer at Aix-en-Provence, and in the libraries of the University of Adelaide, Institute of Development Studies at the University of Sussex, School of Oriental and African Studies, London, and Bibliothèque Nationale, Paris. I would like to thank the staffs of all those libraries for their assistance, particularly Mlle Lucette Vachier of the French National Archives and Howard Coxon at the University of Adelaide. Others who gave important help in obtaining materials were Peter Limqueco, Irene Norlund and Raymond Feddema.

I would also like to thank those who have made useful comments on parts of the work, including David Marr, Bruce McFarlane, Suzy Paine and Christine White, and those who have provided other sorts of inspiration from time to time, especially Prue Kerr, Chris Gregory, Geoff Harcourt, John Sender and Sheila Smith. None of the above-mentioned people, however, bear responsibility for the final product.

Sources

I have used four main types of material in preparing this book: (i) material gathered during my visits to Vietnam; (ii) material from the French National Archives and official US documents contained in the *Declassified Documents Reference System*; (iii) translations of Vietnamese language documents and radio broadcasts published by the Joint Publications Research Service in *Translations on Vietnam* (later *Vietnam Report*); the BBC in *Summary of World Broadcasts* (Far East); and USAID in its *Vietnamese Documents and Research Notes*; (iv) Vietnamese publications, including Vietnamese language publications, English and French translations of Vietnamese works and materials (especially statistical publications) in more than one language. It is necessary to say something about the quality and reliability of these sources.

(i) Material gathered in Vietnam Owing to the very short time available, it was necessary to narrow the focus of enquiry to the problems of southern Vietnamese agricultural development in order to try to get more depth of information. In Hanoi I visited the Ministry of Agriculture, a suburban cooperative and the Agricultural University and met Nguyen Huu Tho (agricultural editor of the Party newspaper *Nhan Dan*) and Dao Van Tap (director of the Social Sciences Commission). However, my requests to visit the State Planning Commission, the Price Commission and Ministry for Home Trade could not be met. In the south I met with Ministry of Agriculture officials in Ho Chi Minh City, Dong Nai, Song Be, Ben Tre and Long An provinces, visited a number of agricultural enterprises and met an official from the local branch of the Price Commission. The results of these meetings varied considerably in terms of my research requirements: the persons I met were often unable to provide the sort of information I wanted, usually because they did not have relevant data. In some cases the time allotted was insufficient to get through my questionnaire or to query apparent inconsistencies. This meant some of the information collected could

not be used. I believe the main cause of these problems was inadequate contact between myself and the sponsoring institution in Vietnam before the visit. Hopefully the gradual restoration of Vietnam's links with the West which has occurred since 1985 will lead to better preparation being possible for scholars in the future.

(ii) Archives The research for Chapter 2 was carried out mainly at the Dépôt des Archives d'Outre-Mer of the French National Archives in Aix-en-Provence. These contain the archives of the French administration in Indo-China. Information on the economy of Vietnam during the colonial period can be found chiefly in three collections:

(a) Fonds des Amiraux et du Gouvernement général;
(b) Fonds de la Direction des Affaires économiques du Gouvernement général (known as the Service économique);
(c) Conseiller aux Affaires économiques (Saigon). In addition, there are a large number of official publications from both the central Government and the residencies of Tonkin, Annam and Cochin-China.

Unfortunately there are many gaps in these archives. Exigencies of war and poor storage conditions prior to their removal to France have taken a toll on the documents. There are also many issues missing from the series of official publications and wherever possible I have supplemented these from the Bibliothèque Nationale in Paris. Other documents may be available in the French National Archives in Paris and in Vietnam itself, but these will have to await further research.

The other main archival source, which I have used extensively in Chapter 3, is the US Government *Declassified Documents Reference System*, available on microfiche. This contains a vast number of documents originating from sources such as the Defense Department, State Department and the CIA concerning Vietnam and the Vietnam War, mostly dating from the 1960s. Economic development of Vietnam was a rather secondary issue for the authors of these documents, so that economic data tends to be scattered and fragmentary. Nevertheless, it provides a rich source, provided it is understood that in compiling economic data, US officials did not have access to some areas of the country and, moreover, that the range of comments was often limited by policy considerations of the US Government.

(iii) Translated documents Both JPRS and the BBC's *Summary of*

World Broadcasts provide translations of Vietnamese documents and broadcasts. The former is the more comprehensive source since it includes translations of selected articles in the main political and economic journals. Apart from the difficulty of having to rely on translations, the comments made below about Vietnamese publications also apply. Nevertheless, the two constitute an extremely valuable source given the limited accessibility of Vietnamese language materials to Westerners.

(iv) Vietnamese publications   These include publications of the former Republic of Vietnam (Government of South Vietnam), the Democratic Republic of Vietnam (North Vietnam) and the present Socialist Republic of Vietnam. In the case of the former RVN there is a wide range of published statistics. The reliability of these is questionable, however, particularly those collected by the understaffed National Institute of Statistics while National Bank figures are regarded as more reliable. However, in some areas, for example, population figures and agricultural output, the wartime conditions only served to exacerbate the typical problems of collecting and interpreting statistical data of Third World countries. Statistical publications from the socialist side are not nearly as comprehensive – for example they do not include data on foreign aid, balance of payments or price movements though these can sometimes be gleaned from other sources. They suffer from similar inconsistencies and hiatuses as the Southern data – a situation which is not helped by the near total absence of notes and definitions. I have tried to make the reader aware of these problems in the text where necessary.

MELANIE BERESFORD
May 1988

Terms and Abbreviations

VIETNAMESE REGIONS

In this book 'North' and 'South' (with capital letters) refer to the territories of the former Democratic Republic of Vietnam and Republic of Vietnam respectively. The use of 'north', 'centre' and 'south' refers to the three regional divisions known in colonial times as Tonkin, Annam and Cochin-China. The Vietnamese names for these regions – Bac Bo, Trung Bo and Nam Bo – are also sometimes used.

VIETNAMESE SCRIPT

The written language contains a number of diacritical marks used to distinguish pronunciation tones. These are omitted from Vietnamese words in this book.

ABBREVIATIONS

ARVN	Army of the Republic of Vietnam
CIA	Central Intelligence Agency
CIP	Commercial Import Program
CMEA	Council for Mutual Economic Assistance
CPV	see VCP
DDRS	Declassified Documents Reference System
DRV	Democratic Republic of Vietnam
FAO	United Nations, Food and Agricultural Organisation
FLPH	Foreign Languages Publishing House
IBRD	International Bank for Reconstruction and Development (also World Bank)
IDEO	Imprimerie d'Extrême-Orient
IDS	Institute of Development Studies, University of Sussex
ILO	International Labour Organisation
IMF	International Monetary Fund
JPRS	Joint Publications Research Service
NEZ	New Economic Zone
NLF	National Front for the Liberation of South Vietnam

RVN	Republic of Vietnam
SIPRI	Stockholm International Peace Research Institute
SRV	Socialist Republic of Vietnam
SWB	Summary of World Broadcasts
USAID	United States Agency for International Development
VCP	Vietnamese Communist Party

NORTHERN
VIETNAM

SOUTHERN
VIETNAM

1 Introduction

Unifying parts of a nation with dissimilar or antagonistic socio-economic profiles is a thorny problem. This book is a case study of an Asian socialist country grappling with the absorption of a large capitalist region. Vietnam is not the only country facing such problems. In the post-war period, either directly or indirectly as a result of the carving up of the globe into 'spheres of influence' of capitalism and socialism, a number of previously unified nation states have found themselves divided in two. Defeated Germany was the first to be split, but in the majority of cases (China–Taiwan, North and South Korea, North and South Vietnam), the divisions have come about because the aspirations of local peoples did not coincide with the interests of the Potsdam Conference of the Allied Powers. As far as Asia was concerned, these interests were largely based on the pre-war colonial status quo. In each case, national liberation movements were opposed by the colonial powers, including the United States, both for imperial reasons and out of fear of their socialist content. From the wars which followed, divided states emerged – with one part sustained by US aid and/or military intervention, the other part under communist rule.

National reunification has been a primary goal on both sides of the dividing line in all these countries, but Vietnam has been the only one able to make it a reality, albeit after a long and costly civil war. For the Chinese, Koreans and Germans it remains a distant hope, but the Vietnamese experience is still relevant to them: the Vietnamese reunification process after 1975 has not been smooth and may hold many lessons, especially concerning the imposition of a socio-economic model derived from the experience of one 'half' on the other.

There is also the case of Hong Kong and Macau, two colonies hived off from Chinese territory by the Europeans, but now facing imminent reabsorption. Taking into account the difference in sizes involved, as compared with the two halves of Vietnam, lessons may yet be drawn as to the likely impact upon one another of the two social and economic systems of communist China and capitalist Hong Kong and Macau. The Chinese approach to Hong Kong has been based on the desirability of maintaining the former colony as a separate economic entity without any attempt to achieve a 'socialist transformation' for at least fifty years. It has been argued that something along these lines would

1

have been a better option for the Vietnamese[1] and in so far as unification involved a straightforward attempt to impose a 'Northern model' on the very different South, this is certainly so. However, maintenance of a clear separation may have generated further obstacles to eventual unification. Moreover, any effort to maintain newly absorbed areas, as 'capitalist enclaves' within a 'socialist body' is unlikely to succeed if governments permit movement of personnel and investment between the zones. Given that a major war objective of the Communists was reunification, an extended separation was probably not a realistic option. In the event, a certain *de facto* autonomy has emerged in the Vietnamese case, allowing a more gradual transition to take place.

The reunification of Vietnam is not only of interest in comparison with other divided states. One key area for study is the impact of unification on the development of socialism. A major focus of the research for this book was on the efforts of the post-1975 government to effect the 'socialist transformation' of Southern Vietnam's capitalist economy and, conversely, the impact of the market system of the South upon the 'traditional' socialism of the North.

While it is possible, after seventy years' experience, to identify a number of systematic processes in the socialist economies, it remains true that each one has also developed unique institutions. Each society has constructed its socialist system on the basis of a given historical development embodied in its class structure, level of industrialisation and cultural traditions. The forms socialism takes also depend upon whether the transition is begun in peaceful or violent circumstances, with or without the aid of an indigenous revolutionary movement, and upon the degree of external assistance available. In a country where the transition period of two different regions begins twenty years apart, a society in which classes, economy and culture have developed in different directions, one would expect different institutions to emerge. What happens, then, when the two are merged?

In Vietnam certain cultural and socio-economic differences between North and South pre-dated the formal separation of the two regions in 1954. These differences were accentuated by the subsequent development of mutually antagonistic social systems until 1975 when the American-backed regime of the South was defeated. Given their almost equal economic and demographic weight during these two decades, it was unrealistic to expect that, after 1975, structural tension between the two could be avoided as they sought to adjust to a situation of renewed contact and the imposition of a unified political and economic system.

In this book I have attempted to provide an analysis of this structural tension and the ways in which interaction of the two systems opened up new paths of social development.

THE VIETNAMESE VIEW OF UNIFICATION

April 1975 marked a decisive defeat for any attempt to develop Southern Vietnam mainly within a capitalist framework. Nevertheless, the future socialist development of the region could not be created in a vacuum, but only on the basis of an already existing pattern of social relationships and a certain level of development of productive forces. Since they did not consider these relations and forces conducive to socialism, the leaders of the Vietnamese Communist Party attempted to remould them into a new pattern.

Prior to 1975, the Vietnamese themselves made very little explicit reference to the social and economic problems of unification. In the sphere of social relations, the main view was that the South would follow essentially the same path towards socialism as the North, with due allowance for minor social differences. Evidence from the first four years bears this out. In 1975 leading Political Bureau member Truong Chinh declared that the differences between the two zones were 'conditional and temporary', while the similarities were 'basic and decisive', though it was conceded in the Communist Party's theoretical journal that capitalism had 'struck relatively deep roots in the towns and cities' of the South.[2] Transformation was seen as proceeding in the same stages as earlier in the North: an initial phase of recovery from the most immediately soluble consequences of war, nationalisation of the assets of open collaborators of the Thieu regime, followed by a gradual process of socialisation of the rest of the economy. As in the North, this transformation was expected to be achieved within five years, that is, by the end of the 1976–80 Five Year Plan.[3] It involved the creation of state and joint state-private industries in the modern sector, collectivisation of agriculture and handicraft industries and the attempt to bring domestic circulation of goods under state control.

There is no indication that the leadership regarded any aspect of this process as especially problematical.[4] The published documents of the Fourth Party Congress, held in December 1976 make almost no reference to special problems which might be encountered and the description of the South in the immediate post-war phase is very sketchy indeed:

In the South, socialist transformation has just begun; the exploiting classes remain; the poisons of the enslaving culture and the social evils caused by US neo-colonialism as well as the influence of bourgeois ideology in society remain potent; the reactionaries are still operating against the revolution; the negative aspects of capitalism and the spontaneous character of small-scale production are still to be overcome.[5]

This sketchy (and highly contentious) picture sharply contrasts with the detailed and critical analysis in the same source of the trends in the North Vietnamese economy and society following the destruction wrought by the US bombing campaigns.[6]

In many ways, the lack of detailed analysis of Southern society by the 1976 Party Congress is understandable. It reflects a shortage of trained personnel familiar with conditions in the region, largely as a result of the American-devised 'Phoenix' programme for undermining the Southern communist infrastructure by eliminating cadres and administrators. But there may also have been a feeling that the aspirations of the majority of Southerners would, in any case, lead in the direction proposed, given the prior success of the National Liberation Front in mobilising the support of peasants and urban workers alike. This turned out to be far from the reality.

The *economic* basis of unification of North and South was traditionally encapsulated in the notion of 'economic complementarity'. According to this thesis, the mineral and energy resources of the North would, in a unified future, be complemented by Southern agricultural and light industrial capacity.[7] The dislocating effects of the withdrawal of the American aid prop to the South would, once recovery was under way, be at least partly offset by the exchange of Southern food surpluses for Northern industrial output and raw materials. Economic complementarity would thus provide the basis of a self-reliant industrialisation process.

The theory that lay behind this was based on Marx's reproduction schemes in *Capital* and emphasised that the basis of the social division of labour in predominantly agrarian societies is the 'economic link' between industry and agriculture – more particularly, between production of capital goods and consumer goods[8] – and the necessity to maintain a broad proportionality between these. The addition of Southern agricultural resources to the North's industrial and mining capacity therefore seemed to open enhanced possibilities for a more balanced growth than had been possible under conditions of separation. In fact, the Vietnamese sometimes described the separate development of the two regions as 'distorted'.

Another key assumption of Marxist economic theory as interpreted by the Vietnamese Communists was that industry plays the role of a leading sector in the development process, and within industry, capital goods (which are usually loosely conflated with heavy industry) provide the main impulse to growth. As a corollary of this, Northern Vietnam, with its superior level of industrialisation was expected to provide the main economic impetus after unification and, since industry in the North was predominantly state socialist, the socialist relations of production would also lead the more 'backward' private and collective agricultural economy of the South. The Northern economy was frequently described as a 'strong base' for the implementation of socialism in the whole country.[9]

In the light of subsequent developments, this type of analysis of the 'unification problem' seems over-simplistic: it reduced the problem to a simple extension of the socialist industrialisation process across the whole country, gradually absorbing the 'less developed' sectors (Southern agriculture) into more 'socialist' forms of ownership and distribution. Obstacles to unified development, in this view, become mere technicalities: chronic shortage is due to underdevelopment (lack of industrialisation); lack of transport facilities hold back the development of exchange between North and South. Other factors such as poor agricultural seasons, the US economic blockade, conflict with China and some of the long-term consequences of the war are seen as external constraints on development, beyond the immediate control of the Government. These factors have frequently been used as explanations for the apparent failure of economic policy to generate the expected growth result.

External constraints on growth are important enough, but as argued in this book, the special social conditions of the South have also provided a key obstacle to the simple transfer of a 'Northern model'. These conditions, traced in Chapters 3 and 4, contributed substantially to the economic and political crisis which enveloped the country between 1978 and 1980. Acting in accordance with the policy framework for unification outlined above, the Vietnamese authorities responded to this crisis by stepping up the campaign to increase the rate of socialisation. When this produced none of the desired effects on the State's ability to mobilise agricultural surpluses, and when Vietnam's problems were intensified by the outbreak of war with China, by the outflow of 'boat people' and by the need to support devastated Cambodia, the situation demanded re-evaluation and reform.

The perceived need for change of direction in the South coincided with the exposure of a number of serious weak points in the Northern system itself. This served to bring about considerable re-thinking and debate among Vietnamese economists and policy makers. To explain this, Chapters 5 and 6 are largely devoted to a discussion of the crisis affecting the North in the early post-war years and the directions policy has taken towards overcoming these problems.

In dealing with the problems of development in a reunified country, Vietnamese leaders have found it necessary to address the question of Vietnam's position in the international division of labour. Earlier thinking on the 'economic complementarity' of North and South took place largely within a perspective of 'self-reliant' industrialisation – something which has been common to most socialist countries and especially those whose establishment involved a struggle for national independence and a break with the imperial system. Rightly or wrongly, a perceived lack of benefit to 'Third World' countries from expanding international trade has been a major element in the socialist critique of capitalist-style development. While the Vietnamese did adopt a view which favoured integration into the international economy (both Western and socialist) and in 1977 passed a foreign investment law which they hoped would attract some Western investment, in practice trade and investment policy were not linked to any notion of an international division of labour: trade and investment policies were not based upon specialisation in areas in which Vietnam had an actual or potential comparative advantage, but on the creation of an all-round, self-reliant economic structure to which trade would be virtually incidental – a form of voluntary international cooperation, rather than economic interdependence.

The result of this outlook was that in spite of the importance to its economy of trade in primary products during the colonial period, the DRV from 1955–75 and the SRV built up a wide range of manufacturing industries which, because of the small size of the Vietnamese market, long gestation periods and technical and management problems associated with input shortages, were unable to take advantage of economies of scale. This situation was made worse after 1975 by the failure of the Southern agricultural economy to recover its export capacity. In a situation of acute foreign exchange shortages brought about by withdrawal of US aid from the South and the ending of

Chinese commodity aid to the North, the inability to expand export income was a major contributor to the economic crisis of the late 1970s and early 1980s. This too provoked a rethinking of economic strategy, with increased emphasis placed on development of an international division of labour within CMEA, which Vietnam joined in 1978, and with the West.

How far the process of rethinking and reform in economic policy goes will be a major element influencing the future shape of Vietnamese socialist society. The responsiveness of the Southern economy to the stimulus of reforms will be a major determining factor. Moreover, to the extent that current trends in the growth of Southern agriculture and light industry can be sustained and matched by recovery in a more streamlined Northern industrial sector, the 'economic complementarity' thesis may yet come into its own.

AN ANALYTICAL FRAMEWORK FOR THE UNIFICATION PROCESS

Many of the reforms introduced in Vietnam in the decade since the end of the war are similar to those carried out in a number of other socialist countries, for example, Hungary, China and the Soviet Union. It might be deduced from this that the Vietnamese are simply following a model, or that all socialist societies necessarily follow the same path in the long run. But I argue in this book that while the similarities can indeed be attributed to certain systemic features of these economies and to similar traditions and structures of the Communist Parties, the differences are also important. These differences arise from the unique configuration of each social formation. The power of the State *vis à vis* the social classes needs to be analysed, as do the relations between classes (peasants and workers, for example), and the varying importance of external influences. In a capital-scarce economy like Vietnam, the availability of external assistance becomes crucial in determining the level of accumulation, and is therefore one of the main elements governing the rate of growth, as well as the degree of autarky or openness of the economy. The need for military preparedness also limits the options for choosing an economic development strategy. In Vietnam, unification of North and South has added another set of pressures for change, provided a more complex determination of the economic and political processes of the last decade.

The question of economic unification has both a social and a more narrowly economic dimension. The first concerns the character of the social relations which shape the organisation of production and which are expressed in patterns of distribution and exchange – the class relations of society. The second refers to the process of economic growth itself – the organisation of production (labour process) and reproduction, the accumulation of capital, generation of total economic surplus, technological change, circulation and distribution of goods – the expansion of society's productive forces. The two dimensions are not independent of each other: as Marx pointed out, social relations determine the way in which productive forces are deployed and surplus appropriated; in turn, the development of productive forces transforms social relations. Indeed the interaction between them forms the material basis of the historical process.

In this study of the unification of Vietnam, both dimensions are combined. Since the process of unification takes place on the basis of existing economic and social structures, the approach here also needs to be historical. We begin, in Chapter 2, with the latter part of the colonial period when Vietnam, along with Laos and Cambodia, was ruled by the French as a single unit (though with three subdivisions then known as Cochin-China, Annam and Tonkin). The colonial period saw the gradual expansion of capitalist relations of production in Indo-China as a whole, a process which has been analysed by others.[10] It is the differential impact of these new social relationships on the economic development of the three regions which is the main focus of this chapter. These variations are important because they created the foundations upon which separate development of North and South later took place. Moreover, the question arises as to what extent the separation (in 1954) caused a dislocation to the economic life of the country and a setback to the development process. Dislocation might imply that the economy had previously functioned as a single unit and, in investigating the extent of this unity/separation it became necessary to clarify exactly what is meant by 'economic unification'.

Here again the social and economic dimensions come into play. At one level, it would be possible to claim that socialist production relations were dominant already in 1975 with the change of government in the South. The defeat of the Saigon regime was certainly an important step in that direction, since it put a halt to any systematic development of capitalism in the South for the foreseeable future. However, the practices embedded in a particular set of production relations are not necessarily transformed by the change of a political regime. Sections of Southern society proved capable of resisting the changes which the new, post-1975, government wished to bring about and such resistance was largely responsible for the depth of economic crisis affecting Vietnam in 1977–81. It brought forth both a repressive response and, subsequently, a series of compromises which have created new institutions and practices not hitherto part of the Vietnamese socialist system (as it had developed in the North). One of the most important new aspects has been that commodity relations are no longer seen as 'capitalist' or 'petty bourgeois', but as an essential component of an advanced 'socialist' economy. Many attributes of the old Southern economy which were previously rejected as manifestations of 'neo-colonialism' are now seen in a more positive light. This shift of opinion has also influenced the Government's response to problems facing the Northern state-socialist and collective institutions.

Socialism, like capitalism, allows for a number of different forms of the fundamental social relationships – in capitalism, for example, sharecropping systems can be adapted from a pre-capitalist mode of production to suit the accumulation requirements of capital. Similarly, a socialist economy may contain state, collective and individual (or family) organisation of the labour process. It cannot be presumed, *a priori*, that new, previously untried institutional forms are 'less socialist' than the old ones. Much depends upon what changes are taking place in the forces of production and on the ways in which surplus is appropriated. In the long run, then, unification in the sphere of production relations may lead to a quite different set of socialist institutions and relationships from those of the 'traditional' socialism of the North.

Turning to the dimension of productive forces, unification involves the establishment of a national market – a nationwide system of production, circulation, distribution and exchange. A political entity which contained a number of autarkic economic villages or regions could not be considered economically unified, nor could one in which the economic units, while not autarkic, traded, or engaged in surplus transfer, only with foreign countries rather than with each other (the case of North and South Vietnam between 1958 and 1975). However, though one can conceive of regional economies which are quite autonomous, it is unlikely that unification could ever be absolute. Unevenness of economic growth and relative isolation of some areas may mean low levels of exchange between one part of the economy and another leading to development of centrifugal tendencies (the case in Yugoslavia). Owing to the shape of the country, as well as earlier patterns of development, the northern and southern deltaic plains of

Vietnam to some extent form natural poles around which regional patterns of development might develop further. Inevitably there will be counteracting tendencies to integration of the system of distribution and exchange, although these may also affect Vietnam in other ways than along a North–South divide. ('Traditional' forms are more likely to persist, for example, in remote mountain areas than in the deltaic plains.)

The process of national integration in Vietnam is bound up with that of economic construction and growth, indeed the one implies the other. The theory of economic development employed in this book is broadly derived from Smith and Marx, since this is a type of economic theory which emphasises the importance of the historical processes of accumulation and increasing division of labour as the engines of development, rather than the more static concerns of orthodox theory. However, many economists within the Marxian tradition, as well as orthodoxy, tend to focus on markets as means of resource allocation (or distribution and exchange), forgetting that markets also have a role in the generation of growth. What is distinctive about an approach based on Smith and Marx is that it provides a model of the production and *reproduction* of the economy which shows the circular feedback mechanisms necessary for the production cycle to continue over time. Smith and Marx saw the growth process as simultaneously an extension of the division of labour in production and an expansion of markets, the dynamic impetus imparted to the economy arising from the interactions of the two.

In general, the more advanced the mode of production, the more highly integrated is the system of production and exchange and the less it is characterised by self-sufficiency of economic units (be they individuals, villages or whole regions). Advanced industrial economies, from which Marx and the Marxists thought socialism would finally emerge, are, above all, economies in which the division of labour has developed to such an extent that individuals cannot produce their subsistence requirements independently of the system of exchange; nor, given the degree of specialisation and cooperation within the labour process, can individuals claim any given product as their own. This increasingly social nature of production and reproduction is viewed by Marxists as the material basis for the emergence of socialism, since it comes more and more into conflict with the private appropriation of the surplus product under capitalism.

Vietnamese Communists still look upon their society as being in transition from one in which these aspects of the productive forces are poorly developed to one in which 'large scale socialist production' will be possible. One of the major debates which has developed within the Vietnamese Party has been around the issue of whether social control over the productive forces and social appropriation of economic surpluses can be used to promote a more advanced division of labour (a view strongly influenced by Maoist thinking). The alternative position has been that so long as the labour process remains individual, there will be strong pressures to revert to private systems of appropriation and control, and that any attempt to override this is likely to hamper further development of the productive forces by causing producers to resist entering the market.

A major theme of this book is that events surrounding the attempt to create a unified national economy have given rise to the ascendancy of the second point of view and to a better understanding of the relationship between rising productivity and the breaking down of autarky in production.

DEVELOPMENT AND THE UNIFICATION PROCESS

The development of commodity exchange in Indo-China during the colonial period was unevenly distributed: the area directly under French rule (Cochin-China) tended to receive more capital investment and consequently produced a greater economic surplus than other regions. Some of this surplus was distributed to northern and central Vietnam via the central Government budget. Because of this fiscal transfer and the presumed economic complementarity of the zones, it has been argued that separation in 1954 was economically disastrous – particularly for the more backward North.[11]

In Chapter 2, however, I argue that economic unity was less pronounced before 1954 than is commonly assumed; therefore, the degree of dislocation to the economy caused by separation should not be overestimated. While the division of the country involved the loss of *potential* gains more rapid integration of the Northern and Southern regions, the implication of the *actual* historical development is that the economic foundations laid by the French played an important role in determining the divergent courses of development in the next two decades.

Chapter 3 deals with the separate development of Southern Vietnam between 1955 and 1975. It looks first at the development of social classes in the Republic of Vietnam and the way this affected economic development. The consequences of French withdrawal and American economic assistance are also brought into the analysis, as are the economic effects of the war from 1960 onward. The structure of the Southern Vietnamese economy, as it developed over the two decades, is analysed in order to establish the nature of the productive base upon which contemporary reunification is taking place.

The economic history of South Vietnam during this period has suffered considerable scholarly neglect in favour of political and military history. The few works available tend to adopt a 'dependency' perspective, arguing for the overwhelming importance of American domination of the economy in retarding 'real' development. In contrast, the focus of my argument is on the internal balance of forces, beginning with the colonial legacy and tracing the influence, not only of American intervention, but of the National Front for the Liberation of South Vietnam (NLF) and local capitalists, landlords and the military. Although economic progress was indeed slow, the period saw the start of a social transformation similar to that which took place in South Korea and Taiwan preceding economic 'take off'. The key to this development was intensification of the social division of labour, the extension of the South Vietnamese market and its integration into the international economy.

An important section of this third chapter reviews the possibility that, taken as a whole, the Southern economy produced negative economic surplus between 1955 and 1975. While this result did not lead to high international indebtedness, on account of the availability of US grant aid, the withdrawal of all American economic assistance after 1975 had a dramatic impact. The combination of an entrenched market economy (with high levels of interdependence) and acute shortages of almost all types of goods was politically destabilising for the South and placed strains on the Northern economy which it was ill-equipped to meet.

Economic revival of the South after the war mainly depended on the restoration of the agricultural sector and this is the subject of Chapter 4. Southern agriculture was deemed capable of providing a future surplus for export, for industrial inputs (including urban wage goods) and for national investment purposes. In the mid-1970s, however, the Vietnamese leadership greatly underestimated the nature of the social and economic transformations which had taken place, especially in the crucial Mekong River delta. Land reform had been largely achieved by 1970 and it was thought that relatively minor readjustments would enable collectivisation (following the pattern of the North) to produce the desired increases in outputs and yields. The reasons for the failure of this project are examined as background to the introduction of economic reforms in the 1978–80 period. The chapter poses the question, which can only be partially answered at this stage, of the extent to which the difficulties in the rural sector of the South were responsible for the introduction of these reforms country-wide; that is, for the virtual abandonment of the model of socialist development which had been practised in the North for 25 years. Nevertheless, the ultimate objective of a collectivised rural economy in the South has not been abandoned and I argue that the reforms have in fact increased the likelihood of success in the long run by improving material conditions, creating an integument in which households and collectives can increase their technological level, and eliminating areas of conflicting interests between households, collective managements and the State.

The forms that collectivisation will take are likely to be very different in future. Chapter 5 demonstrates that it was not only the problems of Southern agriculture which led to the economic reforms of 1979–82 and after. Persistently low productivity of the North Vietnamese collective system up to the late 1970s and the implications of reform, not only for improved productivity, but for the aims of eventual socialisation of the economy, are discussed. By making use of comparisons with similar experiences in China in the late 1970s and eighties, the chapter re-examines some of the basic assumptions underlying collectivisation policies – particularly those relating to the division of labour and economies of scale, incentive systems for individual workers and collective units, the appropriation and distribution of surpluses.

The system of collective agriculture originally established in North Vietnam proved incapable of generating the long-term gains in labour productivity necessary to bring forth a rising agricultural surplus which would draw the rural population into an expanding national market. An increased role for household farming and 'unorganised' markets is a way towards greater socialisation of production and distribution. However, there are limitations to the effectiveness of such reforms in generating sustained growth in the agricultural sector in the absence of other changes in the economy.

Some of these limitations are canvassed in Chapter 6 where I suggest that the relative lack of developed 'economic link' between North Vietnamese industry and agriculture was a major factor in the slow rate of recovery of the industrial sector from the devastation wrought by US wartime bombing. Severe disproportionalities were also induced by the 'heavy industry priority' policy which continued to be pursued in the investment allocations of the 1976–80 Plan. Chronic shortages (and accompanying waste) were rendered far more acute than has been seen in other socialist economies by the sharp drop in the availability of non-refundable external resources after 1975. In consequence, the heavy industry sector of the North was not well equipped at the end of the war to carry out the role accorded it by those leaders who accepted the 'economic complementarity' thesis. The ability of the state-socialist sector to dominate the 'commanding heights' of the economy has also been adversely affected.

Reform of the industrial system was set in train after 1979, but in the North this has been slower to take hold than in the South. The reasons may be found in Northern institutional traditions of administrative planning as well as in the sheer difficulty of making rapid alterations to the structure of an industrial economy. In may respects the Southern economy, because of its greater ability to respond to market-style incentives and benefit from the lower marginal capital-output ratios of its agriculture and light industrial sectors, has assumed the more dynamic role in the 1980s.

Some of the threads emerging in the previous chapters are brought together in Chapter 7. It discusses the essential differences between the Northern and Southern economies by 1975 – the extent of the development of production for exchange (as opposed to the own-consumption characteristic of the pre-capitalist mode of production) in the two regions; the ownership and control of means of production; major concentrations of economic power (in particular the appropriation and distribution of economic surpluses) and the impact of these on economic growth patterns. It is argued that the key to successful economic unification of the country must be the creation of a genuinely national market, as opposed to a series of largely semi-autarkic regional and local markets. This will involve both the generalisation of production for exchange (especially in the North where it is so far less developed) and an increasingly sophisticated division of labour as industrialisation proceeds. It will also involve abandonment of the attempt to create an all-round self-reliant industrial sector which in the past has led to excessive concentration of investment in uneconomic large-scale heavy industrial projects. An increasing involvement in the international division of labour should also enable Vietnam to make use of both comparative advantage and potential economies of scale in industrial production and thereby boost its rate of growth.

For the time being, there are considerable political obstacles to the achievement of unity. These lie in the existing power structure, in the ability of provincial and local authorities to operate independently of the central Government due to their relative economic independence, and among bureaucrats whose control over resources is threatened by the reform process.

However, there are signs that the positive impact of reforms on the Southern economy is helping gradually to break down this resistance, and that genuinely new forms of socialist institutions may ultimately emerge. In so far as this does take place it will result not from the unification objectives of the Government but, paradoxically, from reciprocal impact of the two distinctive economic systems of North and South.

2 Political Unity and Economic Separation: the Colonial Period

Jean Lacouture has written of the partition of Vietnam in 1954 that:

> Before the partitioning . . . Viet-Nam certainly had not always been politically united, and the division of the colonial epoch – with Tonkin in the North, Annam in the Centre, and Cochinchina in the South – corresponded quite well to the realities of cultural traditions and collective psychology. But in the economic domain, Vietnamese unity took on overriding importance. . . . To create two political capitals, Hanoi and Saigon, was partially justified, but to break up Viet-Nam's economic unity was to attempt the irrational.

This passage is also cited by Nguyen Tien Hung[1] in the only major work to date which has explicitly dealt with the problem of economic reunification after 1975. Indeed Hung goes a good deal further than Lacouture in asserting that the 'traditional dependence of the North on the South to compensate for its annual food deficit, combined with the failure of the Communist regime to solve the food problem . . .' was the primary reason for the launching of 'total war . . . to conquer the South'. To substantiate this thesis, Hung goes to considerable lengths to detail the 'economic complementarities' between the two regions, focusing in particular on the export of rice from the Mekong delta (in French Cochin-China) to the deficit areas of Tonkin and northern Annam.

My own research has led me to place more emphasis on the political motives for the Vietnamese Communists' goal of national reunification and to suspect that the economic unity of Vietnam under the French has been exaggerated by writers like Lacouture and Hung. Nevertheless, there were important economic relations between the two regions during the French period and their disruption after 1954 will have had consequences for the subsequent patterns of economic development.

The aim of this chapter is to answer three questions: (a) to what extent can we regard Vietnam during the period of French colonial

16

domination as an economic unit; (b) to what extent did the ending of colonial rule and the division of the country into two politically and economically separate zones lead to a dislocation of the national economy and how did this affect subsequent development or create problems of reintegration; (c) what lessons, if any, can be drawn from the experience of the management of the national economy as a single unit (though divided into three sub-regions and having the addition of Laos and Cambodia)? It is not intended that the chapter should cover all aspects of Vietnamese economic development prior to the 1954 division: that would require a major work in itself and detract from the main focus of this book which is the problems associated with unification. Readers will find, then, that some key features of the economy are not dealt with here.

DEVELOPMENT OF A NATIONAL ECONOMY

The answer to the first question posed above is that there is only a very limited extent to which we can regard Vietnam as an economic, rather than a political, unit prior to 1954. This arises both from the pre-capitalist forms of production which prevailed in the rural areas and constituted the means of subsistence of the great bulk of the peasant population, and from the way in which the market economy itself had developed under French domination – as an export-orientated system based on the two major ports of Haiphong and Saigon. In spite of the oft-alleged complementarity of Northern and Southern Vietnamese economies, I have found that the French took very little advantage of it and that in so far as greater integration of the village-based economic units into the larger whole took place, this was on a regional basis. The market economy of the Mekong delta and southern Central Vietnam (the areas called by the French Cochin-China and Southern Annam) were strongly linked to the southern capital, Saigon. The orientation of the Red River delta, its surrounding highlands and Central Vietnam, as far south as Tourane (Da Nang), was towards Hanoi and Haiphong.[2]

Evidence for the first part of my contention, that the limited nature of the development of a national economy is attributable to pre-capitalist forms of production, is found mainly in the study by Pierre Gourou, of the peasantry of the Red River delta.[3] This detailed study, carried out during 1936, showed that the villages of the delta area were, for the most part, self-sufficient production and consumption units. Trade between these villages, though vigorous and often involving a high degree of product specialisation, was at the same time miniscule compared to the combined production of the villages. Items traded were those necessities which peasant households were unable to produce for themselves. For example, owing to the shortage of pasture land in the delta, cattle were imported from the Lang Son area, from Kwangsi (in southern China) and from Thanh Hoa province (northern Annam). Peasants often resold these draught cattle as soon as their work was done because they could not afford to keep them. Some delta villages specialised in certain artisan industries (weaving, embroidery, carpentry, etc.), or cottage handicraft industries (basket weaving, food processing, hat making, etc.), although income from these was normally supplementary to farm income rather than a primary source. Gourou summarised the situation thus:

> The 6 500 000 peasants of the Tonkin delta live in a closed economy; they buy and sell little; a family subsists by consuming its own products and reduces by a maximum the needs which it cannot satisfy without expenditure. Also, the delta, taken as a whole, undertakes very small exchanges with the surrounding regions.[4]

Robequain confirms, from his study of Thanh Hoa province, that a similar pattern prevailed in the northern Annam deltas and, given the similarities of production methods, land–labour ratios and social and cultural practices, this is likely to be true for the other Annam delta regions. In Cochin-China, which differed substantially in that many of its cultivated areas had been opened up only since the French occupation,[5] French rule was longer-established and French capital more widely invested in agriculture, the market economy was already more extensive, and most of the traditional craft industries had been heavily affected by import competition.[6]

Outside Cochin-China, peasant participation in a market system which extended beyond the confines of the delta regions was largely confined to the trade in draught animals (mentioned above), salt and construction timber or bamboo. The latter came from the highland regions of Tonkin and Annam and was transported by floating down river to the deltaic plains whence it was sent on to the main markets by coastal shipping or by rail. The use of the river systems and the fact that, before 1936, the railway system was divided into two (northern and southern) regional networks, ensured that this timber trade remained largely regional (see the section on *Domestic Circulation of Goods*, p. 27, for details).

Any tendency of the essential economic autarky of north Vietnamese villages to break down must certainly have received a setback during the anti-French war (1945–54) when the newly formed Democratic Republic of Vietnam (DRV) actively *promoted* autarky as the best means of resistance. The policy was (a) to sabotage French lines of communication and (b) to encourage self-sufficiency in production in DRV-controlled areas. Though inter-zonal trade did begin to grow rapidly after 1952, it was from a low base.[7]

Much more important than the trade in which peasants were engaged, however, was the development by the French of several major export commodities, based on mining in the north and plantation agriculture in the south. In northern Vietnam, coal production, mainly in the region near Hon Gay north-east of Haiphong, was predominant. In 1932 coal provided 89 per cent of total value of Indo-China mining production, although by 1937 this figure had fallen to 63 per cent.[8] Other mineral products of the Tonkin region were zinc, tin, wolfram, antimony, silver, lead, gold and iron ore. Some mining of apatite (phosphate ore) was also carried out in Upper Tonkin, near the Chinese border. Tonkin was the principal mining area, producing 99 per cent of total output in 1923, but only 83 per cent in 1937 (of the remaining 17 per cent, about two-thirds came from the Laotian tin mines). Between 1933 and 1937 an annual average of 1 450 000 tonnes (about two-thirds of production) of anthracite was exported. Of the other mining products, phosphate was the only one for which some domestic use was found. The north also exported some cement (125 000 tonnes in 1937, or 53 per cent of the output of the Société des Ciments Portlands Artificiels de l'Indochine).[9] The only other areas of commerce in which Tonkin and northern Annam could be said to have the major share were in a number of forest products and agricultural crops which, however, were not very strongly developed under the French. These included lac and anise which came from Tonkin and cinnamon and cassava from Annam. Maize, which became an important export-earner by the 1930s due to French farmers' demand for livestock feed, was also exported from Tonkin.

On the other side of the trade ledger, Nam Dinh, Haiphong and Hanoi were centres for the working-up of imported raw cotton and silk, the yarn and fabric then being distributed throughout Tonkin and Annam and as far afield as Cochin-China (see page 20).[10] The textile industry catered to the domestic market and did not expand into export markets during the colonial period.

By far the greatest exporter of agricultural products was Cochin-

China; moreover its export crops gave this region the pre-eminent place in Indo-Chinese foreign trade. This was largely due to rice which, up to 1931, usually represented more than 65 per cent of total Indo-Chinese export values.[11] Cochin-China exported about 80 per cent of this, Cambodia being the other major supplier. After 1932 maize and rubber became more important, contributing about 22 per cent of total export values on average between 1932 and 1936 (the share of rice falling to 49 per cent).[12] Cochin-China was responsible for about half the maize and two-thirds of the rubber. Products exported from southern Annam included pepper, tea, copra (also from Cochin-China) and dried fish. For transporting goods from the Mekong delta the French greatly expanded the system of waterways by building canals which connected the main rice-growing areas directly to Saigon. The railway was extended from Saigon to My Tho in the delta, to Loc Ninh (a major rubber-growing area near the Cambodian border to the north) and to Nha Trang on the Annam coast, passing through the rubber areas on the way. Roads were constructed into the highlands of Annam for the benefit of tea and coffee planters.

In southern Indo-China, particularly in Cochin-China, market relations were more highly developed than in Annam and Tonkin. This meant that in addition to the major export industries, there was also a considerable domestic trade providing consumer goods to the delta region and supplying the industries which grew up around Saigon and Cholon. Apart from rice-milling, these industries included sugar-refining, tobacco, vegetable oils, beverages and textiles, supplying the domestic market. Much of the raw sugar for the first of these was obtained from Annam as well as from within Cochin-China itself. Most industries used locally-produced raw materials, with the noteworthy exception of the small weaving workshops at Cholon which used yarn produced at Nam Dinh and Haiphong from imported raw materials.

The basic picture which emerges is of two regional markets, the strongest being based on the Saigon–Cholon conurbation and the Mekong delta, superimposed upon a predominantly backward rural economy (particularly in the northern and central zones) in which there was little demand for goods which could not be produced by the peasant household itself. However, this should not be taken to imply the existence of a dual economy: a very large proportion of the peasantry did have contact with the market economy and, as several authors have pointed out, the French colonial State did succeed in restructuring village economic units to suit the requirements of French and colonial capital-accumulation (based on taxation and labour mobilisation for public works).[13] Rather, the picture being painted here is one in which the gradual integration of the pre-capitalist Vietnamese society into the colonial capitalist mode of production and into the international economy occurred essentially on a regional basis.

There were, however, some notable exceptions, and in answering the second and third questions posed at the beginning of this chapter, we shall need to consider these exceptions fairly carefully. They will be dealt with under three main headings – budget expenditure, domestic circulation of goods, and the contract labour market. In the first case we shall look at the relative contributions of the three Vietnamese sub-divisions of Indo-China to the budget of the central Government and at the way in which expenditure of this budget was distributed among the regions. The aim here is to establish to what extent budgetary expenditure tended to reinforce or overcome the pattern of separate regional development. Secondly we shall examine the patterns of trade between the three administrative sub-divisions in order to find out whether and to what extent, in spite of the predominant export-orientation of the regional economies, trade was taking place between them. Thirdly, we shall consider an important area of north-south trade, linked to one of Indo-China's three main export commodities – the market for contract labour to work on the Cochin-Chinese rubber plantations. This case is singled out, less because it forms one of the more notorious aspects of French colonial activity, than because the basic economic rationale behind the trade – that of reducing population pressure in the over-crowded northern deltas and opening up new economic areas in the less densely populated Mekong delta and southern uplands – is still pursued today using somewhat different methods. Finally, in the light of the examination of these three areas, we shall attempt to answer the questions posed above.

BUDGETS

For the year 1937 receipts from various taxes for which data are available were distributed as in Table 2.1.[14] Together, these three taxes accounted for 27 per cent of the receipts of the General Budget for that year. The bulk of other receipts came from various import duties, taxes on exports and the consumption of tobacco, and income from sales of salt. No regional breakdown is available for these. However, we can say that the export taxes levied on rice, maize and rubber, which contributed 7.9 per cent of receipts in 1937, originated preponderantly in

Table 2.1   General Budget (calendar year 1937)

Receipts from:	Cochin-China	Annam	Tonkin	Others	Total
			Per cent		
Registration, estates and stamp duty	63.5	4.6	27.3	4.6	100.0
Tax on consumption of alcohol	38.4	11.9	30.9	18.8	100.0
Receipts from the sale of opium (estimated)*	43.1	8.4	38.9	9.6	100.0
Total of these items	49.2	7.9	33.0	9.9	100.0

*Figures are actually shares of opium sales by volume: the assumption is made that the value of sales was distributed in the same proportions.

Source   Gouvernement Général de l'Indochine, *Rapports au Grand Conseil des Intérêts Economiques et Financiers et au Conseil du Gouvernement* (hereafter *Rapports au Grand Conseil*), Hanoi: Imprimerie G. Taupin, 1938.

Cochin-China. Bernard estimated that on average, excluding import duties on goods destined for other parts of the union, Cochin-China contributed about 40 per cent of total rax revenue of the General Budget between 1900 and 1935.[15] When we compare these data with the population distribution of the different regions, as shown by the 1936 census, Cochin-China would appear to have contributed a disproportionately high share of the taxes. Of the 22.5 million population of Indo-China, the share of the different regions is shown in Table 2.2.

The difference of course, is accounted for by the greater prosperity of Cochin-China under the French, relative to the four protectorates. This prosperity was due, in large measure, to the development of rice and rubber plantations by private French capital and to the existence of a large Chinese commercial class in Saigon-Cholon. That this relative prosperity extended to the indigenous population to some extent as well, is borne out by the latter's proportionately greater contributions to the (native) alcohol-consumption tax and can be attributed to the higher land–labour ratio of Cochin-China. According to Bernard's estimates, in 1931 Cochin-China contributed about 31 per cent of

Table 2.2 Population of Indo-China in
1936

	m.	%
Cochin-China	4.4	19.6
Annam	5.6	24.9
Tonkin	8.6	38.2
Others	3.9	17.3

Source Archives of the Service
économique, Caisse 35, Carton 238.

output value of Indo-China, compared with Annam's 22 per cent and Tonkin's 34 per cent.[16] This was in a year in which the effects of the Depression had greatly reduced Cochin-China's income from export crops and its share would have been higher in more normal times. Estimates of average annual per capita consumption of certain products for the years 1938 and 1939 are as shown in the following table.[17]

	Cochin-China	Tonkin
Paddy (kg)	*323.0*	*253.0*
Electricity (kWh)	*7.2*	*2.1*
Native alcohol (l.)	*3.0*	*1.4*
Salt (kg)	*13.2*	*5.0*

The importance of these figures on the relatively weightier contribution of southern Vietnam to the General Budget of the French Indo-Chinese colony, lies in its potential contribution to the development of the colony as a whole. Such a contribution could be made via the mechanism of budget expenditure, particularly on the creation of an economic infrastructure, towards an integrated national economy for Vietnam. Unification could be achieved both at the financial level, through surplus transfer from the more prosperous south, and through the promotion of nationwide commodity circulation.

As far as unification of the market is concerned, there is little evidence of an effort in this direction. Nearly 40 per cent of new public works expenditure in the three regions between 1900 and 1929 was on the railway networks, but the line linking the two major networks of Hanoi–Tourane and Saigon–Nha Trang (a gap of over 500 kilometres) was not even begun until 1934. The second largest item of expenditure on public works (20 per cent of the total) was for the irrigation and inland navigation systems of southern Indo-China which were chiefly concerned with the development of the rice export trade of Cochin-China and Cambodia. A further 15 per cent went on road building, and by 1937 this was by far the largest item,[18] although at the end of that year the total length of bitumen road in Indo-China was still 13 km less than that of the old Mandarin road from Hanoi to Saigon.[19]

Thus the main thrust of colonial public works was towards the development of the regional economies and of their external trade; that is, the accumulation requirements of private French capital. The primary economic purpose of the infrastructure built by the French before the Second World War was the development of plantation and mining sectors and of trade with southern China (via the Yunnan–Haiphong railway[20] and the Port of Haiphong–Hong Kong–Canton route). It was here that the importance of the greater taxability of Cochin-China asserted itself.

During the first three decades of the century, public works expenditure was distributed more or less in accordance with the population ratios of the three countries – Table 2.3. I say 'more or less' because I do not have population distribution data for the whole period. The

Table 2.3 Expenditure from General Budget and loans on public works by region 1900–29

	Cochin-China	Annam	Tonkin	Total*
	Per cent			
New public works				
Railways	20.0	35.7	42.7	98.4
Roads	11.0	27.9	25.0	63.9
Hydraulics, etc.	41.7	18.0	34.7	94.4
Ports	52.6	11.8	33.9	98.3
Buildings	19.1	20.3	39.6	79.0
Sewage, etc.	11.6	30.8	27.5	69.9
Other	27.2	24.8	23.5	75.5
Maintenance	20.3	27.5	27.2	75.0
Total	23.9	27.2	34.6	82.1

*Excluding Laos and Cambodia.
Source *Rapports au Grand Conseil*, 1930, pp. 696–7.

divergences from this rough proportionality occur in the case of hydraulics and inland navigation which, as we have already noted, were largely orientated towards the rice export trade of Cochin-China; ports, where expenditure was heavily biased in favour of the two major ones of Saigon and Haiphong; and in sewerage and health establishments where Annam is relatively favoured.

However, population distribution alone cannot account for the apportionment of expenditure on other public works. In the case of railways, for example, the share of Annam is probably explained by the sheer distances involved in the construction of the Annam sections of the Hanoi–Tourane and Saigon–Nha Trang railways. The same can be said about road building, the other major item. Indeed the much higher share of Annam shown in Table 2.4 is largely accounted for by the resumption of railway construction on the Trans Indo-China in 1934. However, taken as a whole, the public works expenditure of the central Government was a rather small proportion of its total. Moreover, the poor state of these works towards the end of French rule, after US Air Force bombing of the railway line during the Second World War and subsequent sabotage by the Viet Minh during the First Indo-China War (1945–54), meant that their contribution towards developing an integrated national economy was small before 1954.

Table 2.4   Public works expenditure by region 1900–35

	Cochin-China		Annam		Tonkin		Total	
	$ICm.	%	$ICm.	%	$ICm.	%	$ICm.	%
General budget	54.5	25.4	59.5	27.8	57.9	27.0	214.3	100.0
Foreign loans	30.4	15.9	78.2	41.0	62.8	32.9	190.6	100.0
Total	84.9	21.0	137.7	34.0	120.7	29.8	404.9	100.0

Source   P. Bernard, *Nouveaux Aspects du Problème Économique Indochinois* Paris: Fernand Sorlot, 1937) p. 21.

Redistribution of public works expenditure was undertaken, with a view to developing the export potentials of Annam and Tonkin, Laos and Cambodia. This is particularly evident in the construction of roads and railways serving the mining and plantation areas of these four regions and connecting them with the two major centres. Other considerations were more strategic, as in the construction of railways towards the Chinese and Siamese borders; the latter were also important trading partners of Indo-China.[21]

The amounts involved which are measurable with the available data were rather small. In 1937 public works comprised only 14 per cent of total expenditure of the General Budget,[22] although these projects represented a rather higher proportion of total Government expenditure (averaging 18–20 per cent between 1900 and 1939), as many were financed by foreign borrowing which was not included in budget figures.[23] It is not possible to say whether similar redirection of funds took place in other areas of Government expenditure, for example in education (2 per cent of total expenditure in 1937),[24] the agricultural service, health (0.73 per cent of total expenditure in 1937), etc.

The lion's share of spending by the French colonial regime was devoted to administration, policing the colony, debt service and a quota paid to the Government of France – factors which have very little to do with the subject matter of this chapter.[25] However, some idea of the overall importance of State investment in public works via the budget mechanism can be gained from data provided by Bernard.[26] What concerns us here is not so much the impact of French colonialism on the economic development of Indo-China, but the extent to which Cochin-China's budgetary contributions to the rest of the country affected this development process. Table 2.4 showed that the budget provided just over half of the finance for public works between 1900 and 1935. The figure of 214.3 million Indo-Chinese piastres compares with 190 million piastres public investment financed by foreign loans plus, according to Bernard's estimate, a total of 800 million piastres of private investment for the period 1890–1931. Thus about 18 per cent of total investment appears to have come from the central budget. Based on the relative shares of receipts and expenditures given above, it can be estimated that the amount of Cochin-China's subsidy to the rest of Vietnam was roughly 15 per cent of this, or less than 3 per cent of total public and private investment.

One other way in which economic surplus was redistributed via the General Budget was through subsidies to local budgets. According to Andrus,[27] these were divided between Annam, Tonkin and Laos in that order. (Note, however, that in 1930 these subsidies accounted for as much as 18 per cent of total receipts of the Cochin-China local budget.)[28] Subsidies to local budgets were an average of 12 per cent of General Budget expenditure in 1932–6 and 1940–1.[29] In 1937–9 they accounted for 2–20 per cent of local budget receipts for Tonkin and 14–

33 per cent in the case of Annam.[30] Nearly 60 per cent of the subsidy was used in 1938 to finance the *Garde indigène*.[31]

DOMESTIC CIRCULATION OF GOODS

In his famous study of the peasantry of the Red River delta, Pierre Gourou[32] pointed out that while the circulation of goods within and between the villages of the delta was energetic and prolific, the amounts involved were small when compared with both the total commerce of the region (including the urban centres) and the total production of the villages themselves. We know from other sources that the external trade of Indo-China was considerable, but little is known of the trading relations at the intermediate level. This trade was largely dominated by Chinese based in Cholon, Haiphong, Hanoi and other major towns. From our point of view, the aspect of the trade which particularly concerns us is that between the different regions of Vietnam – Cochin-China, Annam and Tonkin – and the extent to which this had developed into a genuine national trading network rather than a series of regional networks.

Collecting information on the subject is, to say the least, difficult. The French authorities seem to have concerned themselves very little with it, being much more interested in the development of foreign trade in which French capital was primarily involved. Therefore, the data had to be gleaned from secondary tables almost incidentally inserted in publications concerned with the external trade, or from vast tables of data giving the minutiae of arrivals and departures at every station along the railway line, etc. Moreover, there exist in the French archives very few surviving issues of the relevant publications, so only a sketchy idea of the historical development of this trade can be obtained.[33]

1. Coastal Shipping

The bulk of inter-regional trade was carried out via coastal shipping – chiefly using junks and sampans. The Chambers of Commerce of the ports of Haiphong and Saigon published some statistics of this trade, inasmuch as it concerned their own ports, and given that these two are by far the most important in the country, we can obtain some idea of the nature of the trade from these data.

For the port of Haiphong, some figures are available for the years 1936 and 1937. The figures are given only by volume, so it has not been possible to determine the relative value of coastal trade in the total trade of the port. In any case such a calculation would involve considerable double counting, since much of the trade clearly involves the transit of goods destined for or coming from the external sector (this is especially true of rice and maize).

From Table 2.5 it can be seen that the vast majority of imports into Haiphong came from within Tonkin itself. Apart from coal, most of which would have been for domestic consumption rather than international trade, other major products here are rice and maize – partly destined for export and partly for urban consumption. Ceramics, fibres, dyes and tannins (the fibre consisted chiefly of reeds for the local basketry industry) were others. The main imports from Annam were timber for construction purposes and salt, along with some cereals, fruit and nuts. Most of these would have come from northern Annam (the provinces of Thanh Hoa, Nghe An and Ha Tinh) which had fairly strong traditional trading relations with the Red River delta. Imports from southern Vietnam were, to say the least, feeble. Compared with the size of the rice surplus exported from Cochin-China to the rest of the world (1.7 million tonnes), recorded shipments to the chronic rice-deficit area of Tonkin were minimal in 1936. Of the other products, petroleum products and sugar formed a sizeable proportion.[34]

On the export side, coal formed the preponderant share of exports to the other two regions alongside cement from the Haiphong cement works. In terms of value, however, textiles were also an important component of this trade. Apart from these and chemical products (chiefly salt), the export of goods from Haiphong to southern Vietnam looks very tiny indeed.[35]

1936 is possibly not a very good year to use, since it is towards the tail-end of the Great Depression and shipping activity generally was low in Indo-China that year. However, the comparative figures given in Table 2.6 show that difference from other years in the period 1927–37 is mainly on the export side.

The other main sources of data on the coastal trade is from the Saigon Chamber of Commerce for the year 1922 (Table 2.7). The apparent weakness shown in this table of the trade within Cochin-China itself is somewhat misleading since the importance of the inland waterways in that region far overshadows that of coastal shipping. I have been unable to find any data concerning the former, however. Of those products which were traded within the region via coastal ship-

Table 2.5   Coastal trade of Haiphong in 1936 by region (tonnes)

Product	Arrive from Tonkin	Depart to Tonkin	Arrive from Annam	Depart to Annam	Arrive from Cochin-China	Depart to Cochin-China
Live animals	5	15	2 013	–	–	6
Animal products	18	12	363	63	154	8
Fish and fish products	153	2	200	3	49	10
Bone, tusks and tortoiseshell	–	259	41	–	37	–
Cereal and products	45 274	7 073	2 768	1 299	7 014	589
Fruit and nuts	48	1 428	1 854	3	1 044	407
Plantation crops	279	846	1 103	183	2 529	702
Vegetable oils	354	66	147	24	240	312
Medicinal plants	41	–	116	48	21	98
Timber	764	–	16 428	11	147	119
Fibres	2 817	2 809	980	22	–	52
Dyes and tannins	2 021	30	3	–	–	5
Beverages	4	–	–	298	64	258
Misc. vegetable products	72	–	188	101	66	150
Stone, cement, combustible minerals	163 441	11 011	–	16 548	1 432	36 444
Metals	200	–	56	246	426	223
Chemical products	183	11 259	12 839	202	58	8 866
Manufactured dyes	–	–	–	1	–	4
Colouring	3	–	–	68	9	92
Misc. processed goods	184	1 318	22	146	116	233
Ceramics	3 587	–	7	29	54	101
Glass and crystal	115	–	61	27	121	1 107
Yarn	–	743	–	364	19	765
Fabrics	151	–	82	805	586	1 061
Paper products	359	–	5	368	168	997
Skins	3	2	–	2	19	8
Metal manufactures	60	–	181	163	690	658
Arms and munitions	–	–	–	13	4	77
Furniture	2	–	122	–	46	11
Wooden articles	–	–	582	14	366	137
Musical instruments	–	–	–	1	4	5
Basketry, etc.	1 018	11	79	22	4	12
Misc. manufactured goods	2	7	57	109	1 851	1 268
Totals	221 162	36 889	55 872	21 185	15 685	54 717

Source Port of Haiphong Chamber of Commerce, *Statistiques Commerciales 1936* (Haiphong: IDEO, 1937).

Table 2.6   Port of Haiphong: imports and exports to Annam and Cochin-China and to the rest of the world

| | Annam and Cochin-China | | World |
	tonnes	%	tonnes
Imports from:			
1927–36 average	63 990	26.9	237 994
1937	74 558	25.9	288 174
Exports to:			
1927–36 average	99 942	14.6	683 154
1937	113 588	12.3	922 083

Source   Port of Haiphong Chamber of Commerce, *Statistiques Commerciales 1937* (Haiphong: IDEO, 1938) pp. 70–71.

ping, salt was by far the most important (4715 tonnes imported and 29 384 exported). Rice and fish products are the others. The chief products exported from Saigon to Annam (tonnes) were ceramics and glass (14 214) and petroleum products (4095); the chief imports from that region were fish products (12 186), stones, earths, combustible minerals (11 674) – of which limestone comprised 4139 – salt (3004), fertiliser of all kinds (2345), sugar (1872) and oil cake (1343). Again, it is to be expected that the bulk of this trade concerned the southern Annamese ports of Tourane (Da Nang), Qui Nhon, Nha Trang, Phan Rang, although no figures are available to verify this.

The trade with Tonkin was very lop-sided. In 1922 Cochin-China imported from Tonkin (tonnes) coal, 56 472; lime, cement and plaster, 16 547; miscellaneous manufactures (including textiles, wooden articles, basketry), 3181; matches, 1682 – the first two categories alone accounting for 90 per cent of the total volume. In return, Cochin-China exported to Tonkin (tonnes) coal, 1920; petroleum products, 1116; salt, 1100; and copra, 856 – these four products accounting for two-thirds of total tonnage. Rice which, on the basis of modern accepted wisdom, might be expected to form a substantial part of such a trade, was shipped in rather small quantities.[36]

It has been possible to obtain some idea of the value composition of the coastal trade of Vietnam in 1922. Thus, taking only some of the most important products, we can calculate the values for coastal trade

Table 2.7   Port of Saigon: coastal trade by region in 1922

Product	Arrive	Depart	Arrive	Depart	Arrive	Depart
	Cochin-China		Annam		Tonkin	
Live animals (head)	11 262	–	12	–	3 043	–
	tonnes	tonnes	tonnes	tonnes	tonnes	tonnes
Animal products	149	82	3 141	15	36	14
Fish and fish products	883	1 767	12 186	55	7	19
Tusks, bone, shell, etc.	23	3	5	–	–	37
Cereals and cereal products	1 668	369	1 628	450	686	514
Fruit and nuts	161	142	462	17	50	1 585
Plantation products	578	662	2 074	83	224	60
Vegetable oils and timber	129	1 017	885	54	463	449
Yarn and fibre	94	134	60	84	6	39
Dyes and tannins	7	8	–	20	–	32
Misc. vegetable products	241	149	1 388	139	85	5
Beverages	189	113	2	118	101	216
Stones, coal, earth	814	397	11 674	4 229	73 488	2 215
Metals	–	10	660	577	164	314
Chemical products	4 715	29 385	3 004	228	962	1 120
Manufactured dyes	–	1	–	5	21	4
Misc. processed goods	350	300	127	14 437	1 530	631
Misc. manufactured goods	100	116	698	125	3 181	325
Total (tonnes)	10 101	34 654	37 994	20 636	81 004	7 579

Source   Saigon Chamber of Commerce, *Situation Commerciale 1922*, (Saigon: Imprimerie Nouvelle Albert Portail, 1924) pp. 75–9 and 157–61.

in and out of Saigon shown in Table 2.8. Some other products of small volume, but high unit value, are not included here because of lack of data. They include textiles, yarns and tree products like cinnamon, tea, pepper. It is known that the weaving workshops of Cholon relied almost exclusively on yarn from the Nam Dinh and Haiphong mills.[37]

On the whole, these data tend to confirm the impression from Haiphong that among the many products traded between northern and southern Vietnam, few were of major significance during the colonial

Table 2.8   Value of inter-regional coastal trade via Saigon, 1922

Product	Arrive Cochin-China	Depart Cochin-China	Arrive Annam	Depart Annam	Arrive Tonkin	Depart Tonkin
	French francs 000s					
Live animals	1 689.3				456.4	
Fish products	433.2		5 977.9			
Sugar	520.3		2 472.3			
Lime and cement			655.5		2 620.7	
Coal					2 773.9	
Petroleum products				2 475.5		674.6
Salt	472.1	2 941.9	300.7			110.1
Copra						856.0
Matches					4 706.8	

Sources Calculated from Table 2.7 and Gouvernement Général de
l'Indochine, Administration des Douanes et Régies, *Rapport sur la
Navigation et le Mouvement Commerciale de l'Indochine pendant l'année 1922*
(Hanoi-Haiphong: IDEO, 1928) pp. 89–91.
Note Blank spaces indicate either no data available or sum is less than
100 000 French francs.

period. They also confirm a picture of the linking of the southern
Annamese economy to the rich Mekong delta/Saigon region, not only
through trade in traditional products like fish sauce, salt, legumes, etc.,
but through the development of plantation crops by the French,
particularly sugar.

The most surprising result from Tables 2.5–2.8, in terms of the
argument of Nguyen Tien Hung in particular, is the apparent unimpor-
tance of rice transhipments from Cochin-China to the northern part of
the country. The 1936 figures for Haiphong show only 7000 tonnes of
cereals (chiefly rice and maize) arriving from Cochin-China, while the
earlier figures for Saigon show only 514 tonnes departing for Tonkin.
One explanation for this is that much of the rice trade may have been
outside the auspices of the two Chambers of Commerce, or simply not
accurately reported by them. However, both sets of data do confirm the
far greater importance of intra- rather than inter-regional trade.
Nguyen Tien Hung estimated that an average of 200–250 thousand
tonnes were shipped north annually during the French colonial period.[38] Le Chau has also given a figure of 100 000 tonnes per annum

Table 2.9   Rice and paddy carried by coastal trade 1914–45*, tonnes

Year	000	Year	000	Year	000	Year	000
1914	71.2	1922	25.0	1930	69.7	1938	na
1915	69.7	1923	32.5	1931	107.4	1939	na
1916	79.6	1924	52.3	1932	97.5	1940	na
1917	73.0	1925	86.3	1933	91.9	1941	314.2
1918	99.6	1926	69.6	1934	169.3	1942	398.1
1919	37.7	1927	95.0	1935	164.4	1943	421.3
1920	41.4	1928	80.7	1936	101.0	1944	267.3
1921	37.3	1929	74.8	1937	na	1945	74.3

*Includes intra- as well as inter-regional trade in both directions.
Source   *Annuaire Statistique de l'Indochine*, various issues.

shipped from south to north 'before the Second World War'.[39] How-ever, these estimates are not borne out by the data available for the pre-World War II years. Published figures on rice and paddy carried by the *total* coastal trade between 1914 and 1945 are presented in Table 2.9. While they suggest a considerably greater volume than indicated by the data for Haiphong and Saigon ports alone, particularly in 1922, they also indicate that the figure of 200 000 tonnes is only realistic *after* 1939. Archival materials indicate that most of the shipment of rice from the Mekong delta to the north after 1939 was war-related – for provisioning of Japanese and French troops and administration. It seems that other authors, like Le Chau, have made the mistake of assuming that all coastal rice trade was in a north–south direction rather than intra-regional.

2. Railways

As mentioned in the previous section, railway construction took a rather high proportion of the public works expenditure of the colonial Government. However, the railways made very little contribution to the development of north–south trade owing to the fact that the line linking the two sections of the country was not completed until 1936 – only four years before the outbreak of war in the Pacific. Although completion of this line (connecting Tourane with Nha Trang and the southern railway network) was expected to have a stimulatory effect on trade, particularly on the trade in human labour for the rubber plantations of Cochin-China and Cambodia, few substantial results were achieved before the war.

The only data available on use of the north–south railway (Trans Indo-China) are for the years 1936–7 and are set out in Table 2.10. These figures include the whole line from Na Cham on the Chinese border in the north to My Tho in the Mekong delta to the south, not just the section between Hanoi and Saigon. When compared with the volume and intensity on the two separate northern and southern networks in the immediately preceding years, both these sets of figures show a substantial increase (the figures for 1937 are nearly double those for 1934). The increase is partly due to the economic recovery from the Depression and there is no evidence available concerning the extent to which use was made of the north–south link in the late 1930s. The line was not used extensively for the transport of contract labour in these years because of the lack of accommodation, catering and sanitation facilities at embarkation and debarkation points along the line.[40]

Going back to 1928 and 1929, when the northern network stretched from Na Cham to Tourane and the southern network from My Tho to Khanh Hoa (near Nha Trang), we see that the average distance travelled by each passenger ranged from 30 km between Hanoi and the Chinese border to about 55 km between Saigon and Khanh Hoa. The average distance travelled by a tonne of freight ranged from about 25 km between Saigon and My Tho to 240 km between Vinh and Hue. In 1936 the average length of passenger journeys on the unified networks was still only 46 km.[41]

The railway, however, was clearly important for some inter-regional trade, especially between Tonkin and Annam. Of the three most important products transported by the northern network in 1928

Table 2.10   Volume and intensity of traffic on Trans Indo-China Railway in 1936–7

	1936	1937
Passenger traffic		
Passenger kilometres	395 677 000	544 717 000
Intensity of traffic*	186 992	257 427
Freight		
Tonne kilometres	69 813 000	95 640 000
Intensity of traffic†	32 992	45 198

*Passenger kilometres/length of line.
†Tonne kilometres/length of line.
Source   *Rapports au Grand Conseil*, 1938, p. 399.

(construction timber, 38 932 tonnes; salt 23 479 tonnes; rice and paddy, 15 474 tonnes), the net import of timber and salt into Tonkin from Annam amounted to 79 per cent and 70 per cent of total freight in those products respectively. Net export of rice and paddy from Tonkin to Annam amounted to 11 per cent of total freight in that product. On the whole, Tonkin was a net importer of products from Annam, but the balance in Tonkin's favour amounted to only 10 per cent of the total freight carried on the network. It has not been possible to find data on the gross volumes of reciprocal trade involved.

On the southern network, 5 major items of freight can be distinguished, for 1928 (tonnes): rubble (51 849), cut timber (36 894), earth (32 430), gravel (24 608), and lumber (23 494), making up 56 per cent of the total freight. Of these only cut timber and lumber involved any inter-regional trade at all – in both cases, Cochin-China was a net importer from Annam. Net imports of cut timber amounted to 34 per cent of total freight in that product; net imports of uncut logs amounted to 3 per cent of lumber freight. Net imports of all products amounted to 3 per cent of freight carried. The southern network also appears to have had some importance in conveying labour from southern Annam to the Cochin-Chinese rubber plantations[42] – the line crossed the 'Terres Rouges' between 60 and 115 kilometres from Saigon and another branched north to Loc Ninh.

Destruction of the line during World War II and subsequent guerrilla attacks on French communications networks prevented the use of railways as an effective means of regional integration. By December 1948, only 1306 out of 2623 kilometres of state-run railway line in Indo-China were operating. The north–south link was not functional[43] and in fact could not return to use until after 1975.

3. Road Transport

Roads began to play a more important role in the development of commerce in the 1920s with the increase in numbers of automobiles entering the colony. The number of vehicles registered in the three zones (including motorcycles) rose between 1925 and 1929 as shown in Table 2.11. By January 1938, the numbers (excluding motorcycles) were: Cochin-China, 7895; Annam, 2602; Tonkin, 5762.[44] Most of these vehicles disappeared during the Second World War.[45]

It is not surprising that the numbers remained rather small, given the period and the fact that the system of all-weather roads was limited (even though the road system was later described as 'outstanding by

Table 2.11   Registered vehicles 1925–9

	1925	*1927*	*1929*
Cochin-China	5 446	8 183	9 839
Annam	1 034	1 469	1 908
Tonkin	2 886	3 893	4 882

Source   Rapports au Grand Conseil, 1930, p. 581.

Far East standards').[46] In 1926 the colony had no asphalted roads. After that year the length increased quite rapidly, but by the end of 1937 the total was only 2565 km – less than the length of the 'Mandarin Road' from Hanoi to Saigon. By that time, a further 7384 km (of Colonial Routes) were gravelled and 1538 km were classified as passable to automobiles only during the dry season.[47] That the major development of automobile transport occurred in southern Vietnam is attested by data on petrol consumption by automobiles during the 8 months from September 1948 to April 1949, which shows that 86 per cent was used in Cochin-China, 11 per cent in Tonkin and 3 per cent in Annam – although these figures may well be distorted by the wartime conditions prevailing.[48] The main concentrations of road building under the French occurred in the economically important areas of Cochin-China and Tonkin as well as the militarily important areas along the Chinese border. It can hardly be said, on the basis of this information, that the road network made any contribution to an economic relationship between the northern and southern halves of the country.

4. Summary

Before leaving this section, we may conclude that the only area in which north–south trading links had been firmly established was coastal shipping, although even here the shipment of significant quantities would appear to have been confined to a handful of products. In spite of the evident potential for the development of stronger economic ties between the two regions, it would seem that the disruption to this trade which occurred as a result of successive wars and finally the formal division of the country, with cessation of virtually all economic contact after 1956, is not likely in itself to have brought about a fundamental setback to the development of either zone.

Table 2.12 Workforce on Indo-Chinese plantations
1921–47

Year	No. of contract labourers	Source
1921	4 000*	(1)
1927	22 363†	(2)
1928	31 801†	(2)
1929	28 623†	(2)
	32 014§	(3)
1930	31 627†	(2)
1931	9 288†	(2)
1932	8 544†	(2)
1933	4 194†	(2)
1934	9 885†	(2)
1937	14 510¶	(3)
	24 346#	(3)
1938	17 022**	(3)
	28 000††	(1)

*Tonkinese on plantations of southern Indo-China;

†Contract labourers in southern Indo-China;

§Tonkinese and Annamese on agricultural enterprises
in Cochin-China at 1 June 1929;

¶Contract labour on Cochin-China rubber plantations;

#Contract labour in southern Indo-Chinese rubber
plantations;

**Tonkinese and Annamese contract labourers in
Cochin-China plantations at 31 October 1938;

††Contract labourers working in 'red lands' of Indo-
China at end 1938;

Sources (1) Charles Robequain *The Economic
Development of French Indochina* (New York: Oxford
University Press, 1944) p. 214; (2) Figures cited in
Martin J. Murray, *The Development of Capitalism in
Colonial Indochina (1870–1940)* (Berkeley: University
of California Press, 1980) p. 297; (3) *Rapports au
Grand Conseil*, 1929, pp. 425, 413; 1930, pp. 169, 185;
1938, pp. 103–4.

THE CONTRACT LABOUR MARKET

It has been rather difficult to obtain consistent data on the size of the contract labour force in the plantations of Cochin-China. Such data as does exist is fragmentary and for different periods does not always cover the same categories of people (Table 2.12). However, there seems to be little doubt that the ability of the plantations to obtain labour in this way formed the economically most important aspect of north–south trade during the later colonial period.

Because of the rather high land–labour ratio and relative self-sufficiency among the peasants of Cochin-China, the owners of the newly opening-up rubber plantations found it very difficult to obtain an adequate supply of labour within the region itself,[49] although those closest to the railway lines or to the paddy-growing regions could count on a fairly easy supply of labourers in the off-season. The problem lay in obtaining a permanent, all-year round labour force and for this the plantations turned to the most densely populated areas of the country – the deltaic plains of the Red River and the Annam coast. Because of their very low land–labour ratios, these areas were presumed (and still are) to have a labour force surplus to their requirements. At first it was thought that the relatively high wages offered by the plantations would attract from these crowded and poverty-stricken areas a more than adequate labour supply. A tradition of using local contractors (*cai*) already existed in Vietnam for the purpose of supplying *corvée* labour to the court and this system was adapted and put on a free enterprise footing for the supply of indentured labour to the Cochin-Chinese, Cambodian and southern Annam rubber plantations.

Since the colonial Government had its own set of priorities, not always coinciding with those of the plantation owners, it intervened to regulate this trade. Specific measures taken were to restrict recruitment to certain of the most densely populated provinces, so as not to interfere with the programme for opening up the highland areas of Tonkin and Annam themselves for agricultural enterprises and mining, and to impose quotas on the numbers of labourers to be recruited from Annam and avoid creating labour shortages for the government's own public works programme. As the system developed, the Government also provided health care facilities and inspection of conditions – particularly in the case of returning contractees who often were simply dumped at Haiphong harbour in a poor state of health and with no means of travelling to their home villages. In the latter case, however, it was acknowledged in 1930 that the allowed embarkation and debarkation points of Annam (Ben Thuy, near Vinh, Tourane and Qui Nhon) were badly lacking in this type of control as compared with Haiphong.[50]

The plantation workforce expanded rapidly between 1921 and the middle of 1928. Among these, the proportion of contract labourers is not known, but could have been over 80 per cent in some years. While the majority worked on the rubber plantations of Cochin-China, other contract labourers were employed in other types of agricultural enterprise, but in much smaller numbers. A substantial proportion were working in the rubber plantations of Cambodia. From mid-1928 there was a decline in both the numbers of contract labourers and in the total workforce of agricultural enterprises in southern Indo-China. This decline began with the collapse of the Stevenson Plan and the fall of rubber prices which preceded the onset of the Great Depression. In the years after 1930, the numbers working on the plantations underwent a dramatic decline. By 1938 the size of the contract labour force in Cochin-Chinese plantations had not recovered to 1920s levels, although this is accounted for in the official reports by increased recruitment of free labour.[51] There would appear to have been a very rapid expansion indeed during the Second World War: one official report puts the number of labourers working on the principal plantations of Indo-China in 1945 at 60 000. But owing to the development of the movement for political independence and the disturbances created by French efforts to re-establish their control over the country during 1945–6, this figure had been reduced again, to 26 300, by 1947.[52]

It is not at all clear how accurately the official figures reflect the actual size of the plantation labour force. A striking example arises in the data for 1930. Murray cites official figures which give the total size of the contract labour force for southern Indo-China as 31 627, and the total workforce on Cochin-Chinese agricultural enterprises as 49 000, but also cites another source which indicated a workforce on the rubber plantations of Cochin-China alone of 100 000. The latter figure includes the spouses and children who were not under contract, but who often contributed their labour.[53]

The size of the trade in contract labourers (and again the inconsistency of the data) is reflected in the annual records of arrivals at Saigon, departures from the north and repatriations due to termination of contract or ill-health.[54] These figures are given in Table 2.13, from which it is possible to obtain a broad picture of the volume and direction of trade from the mid-1920s to the years before the Second World War. This pattern needs to be explained both by macroecono-

Table 2.13   Arrivals, departures and repatriation of contract labourers
1932–38

Year	Arrivals at Saigon from Tonkin and Annam	Repatria- tions from Saigon	Net	Depar- tures from Tonkin*	Repatria- tions to Tonkin	Net
	(1)	(2)	(3)	(4)	(5)	(6)
1919–22	9 143					
1923	3 846					
1924	3 482					
1925	3 684					
1926	16 861			19 500		
1927	17 606			19 300	1 600	17 700
1928	17 977	4 006	13 971	17 300	3 900	13 400
1929†	7 428	5 150		5 900	5 600	300
1930	10 828	3 816		12 100	10 300	1 800
1931	2 565			2 500	13 000	− 10 500
1932				200	11 000	− 10 800
1933	2 129§			5 900	6 000	− 100
1934	7 449§			7 100	3 600	3 500
				¶	¶	¶
1935–6				6 374	2 235	4 139
1936–7				8 272	3 846	4 424
1937–8				6 992	4 506	2 486

Sources   Columns (1)–(3) except for 1919–22 and 1930–4 and for the years 1935–8 of Columns (4)–(6) see *Rapports au Grand Conseil*, 1929, pp. 418, 423–6; 1930, pp. 172–6; 1936, p. 76; 1938, p. 104. For the years 1926–34 of Columns (4)–(6), see Pierre Gourou *Les Paysans du Delta Tonkinois*, p. 217. Column (1) for 1919–22 and 1930–4 (Murray, *The Development of Capitalism in Colonial Indochina (1870–1940)*) p. 242.
*Including those from north Annam and also 10 000 departing for the Pacific colonies. †Repatriations from Saigon are to Tonkin only. §1932–3 and 1933–4. ¶Figures are for both Tonkin and Annam.

mic factors affecting the demand for labour and, perhaps more importantly from the point of view of future attempts to encourage inter-regional migration in Vietnam, by political economic factors affecting the supply.

The major external factors influencing the increase in demand for plantation labour up to 1928 and again from 1934 to the beginning of the Second World War were the international agreements governing rubber production. These were the Stevenson Plan, which collapsed in 1928 and the London Agreement of 1934, both of which established production quotas for Indo-China based on the size of French demand. Thus, after 1934 French Indo-China was allowed to produce up to 30 000 tonnes. The limit was exceeded by 1936 and a 'restriction tax' had to be paid to the International Committee. For 1938–43, the agreement was renewed and the quota was raised to 60 000 tonnes. But between 1934 and 1938 the effect of the agreement was to discourage the opening up of new plantations.[55] If inter-imperialist rivalries in the rubber market contributed to the rather slow rate of growth of Indo-Chinese rubber production in the pre-war period, the slump in world rubber prices (between 1925 and 1932 prices fell from 73 cents a pound to less than three)[56] was a major factor leading to turnaround from net inflow to net outflow of contract labour between 1931 and 1933.

However, the downturn in net immigration to the rubber plantations is only partially explained by demand conditions. The ability of planters' agents to recruit labour at source depended also on conditions prevailing in Tonkin and Annam. Moreover, the determination of the proportion of labourers renewing their contracts for another three years in the south depended on these conditions as much as upon planters' requirements. Not only did planters complain of labour shortages at times of peak demand,[57] but they were unable to obtain sufficient labour at times of low demand as well.[58] In fact the French colonialists, in looking towards the densely populated areas of northern and central Vietnam to provide the solution to their labour shortage problems, had overlooked the simple fact that during the busy times of the rice-growing calendar, there was no labour surplus at all in these areas. This can be seen indirectly by looking at the seasonal pattern of internal migration of wage labour in the Tonkin delta[59] and of recruitment for public works (road construction, etc.) by the authorities in Tonkin and Annam.[60] It was a factor deriving from the labour-intensive methods of cultivation employed in traditional Vietnamese rice agriculture which meant that the yield of the rice crop was in proportion to the amount of labour applied. For the majority of north and central Vietnamese peasants, who had access to a plot of land either as owners or (more commonly) tenants and sharecroppers, the possibility of obtaining a living from rice cultivation plus, if necessary, seasonal wage labour, was a more attractive proposition than that offered by the labour contractors. It was only in times of poor harvests when large numbers were threatened with actual starvation or, at best, massive indebtedness, that the plantation contractors received increased applications. Thus the increased rate of recruitment in the first half of 1930 compared with 1929 (Table 2.13), in spite of the crisis in the international market, is explained by a poor northern harvest in the autumn of 1929, followed by a drought in the spring of 1930.[61]

Ngo Vinh Long has cited the opinion of a French adviser to the Governor General of the early 1920s that

> The *nhaque* will consent to leave their villages to work only when they are dying of starvation. Therefore, we must come to the bizarre conclusion that the way to remedy the present difficulty [in obtaining labour] is to impoverish the countryside.[62]

This conclusion reflects very well the conflict of interest between colonial capital and the bulk of the Vietnamese population.

From the point of view of the demand of the plantation sector, the problem of high seasonal demand for labour in the northern deltas was compounded by the fundamentally unattractive nature of plantation work from labourers' viewpoint. Not only was the labour process itself quite different from that prevailing in rice cultivation – the pace of work was determined by the requirements of the capitalist owners for profit rather than by the changes of the seasons and the subsistence requirements of the producer – but the conditions of existence of the plantation workers were brutal, to say the least. This last point has been well documented by other authors,[63] but some indication of the effect these conditions had on the labour force can be gleaned from the mortality rates and the numbers of workers breaking their contracts (that is, running away) (Table 2.14).

The mortality rate in 1927 was 5.4 per cent of the workforce.[64] According to Thompson, this was 4–5 times as great as the average for Cochin-China.[65] After this date, the death rate began to decline: in 1928 it was 4.5 per cent and in 1929, 2.8 per cent. The French claimed that the very substantial reduction in 1929 was brought about by the successful anti-malaria campaign in the hill tracts. Indeed, figures indicate a substantial reduction in mortality from then on and this may also be due to increased government regulation of labour conditions. Big strikes had been held in the plantations in the years from 1928 to 1930 and these may have forced a more active government role in worker welfare.

The question of runaways was a constant problem for the planters who, in any case suffered from labour shortages and resented the expense of bringing new, untrained workers from the north.[66] Those

Table 2.14   Workers breaking contract, mortality rate and net loss to
plantation labour force 1919–40

| Year | Workers breaking contract | | Re- captured | Net loss | | Mor- tality | Total net loss |
	No.	%*	No.	No.	%*	%*	%*
1919–							
1922†	1 462		355	1 107			
1923	730		133	597			
1924	847		216	631			
1925	1 081		205	876			
1926	1 653		557	1 096			
1927	3 824	17.1	1 067	2 757	12.3	5.4	17.7
1928	4 484	14.1	1 339	3 038	9.7	4.5	14.2
1929	4 301	15.0	1 935	2 366	8.2	2.8	11.0
1930	2 973	9.4	680	2 293	7.2	2.4	9.6
1931	734	8.0	321	422	4.5	2.0	6.5
1932	487	5.7	337	150	1.8	1.7	3.5
1933	562	13.4	321	241	5.7	2.0	7.7
1934	860§	8.7	353§	503§	5.1§	2.2	7.3
1935		4.6				1.9	
1936		2.5				0.5	
1937		4.5				1.0	
1938		3.9				0.7	
1939		9.0				0.7	
1940						1.2	

*Percentage of contract labour force. †1 January 1919 to 31 December 1922.
§First ten months only.
Sources   *Rapports au Grand Conseil*, 1930, p. 185; Murray, *The Development
of Capitalism in Colonial Indochina (1870–1940)*, p. 297.

who did try to escape were dealt with severely: on 26 May 1917, 206
Tonkinese labourers employed by the Xa Cat plantation in Thu Dau
Mot province (north of Saigon) left the plantation in breach of their
contracts. The French authorities gave chase in order to 'advise' them
to return, in the words of the official report. However, the latter were
met by 'menacing words and gestures on the Honquam road' and the
labourers were therefore put under guard and charged with insulting
behaviour.[67]

In general, the problem was met by using police methods: the
numbers of workers being returned to plantations grew during the
1920s on account of 'improved security methods'.[68] In other parts of
Cochin-China, the problem of how to attach immigrant labour more

firmly to the soil was resolved by constructing village-type labour colonies in which family accommodation replaced barracks and families were given a house, a rice field and a place for ancestral tombs. Government policy in the mid-1930s was to encourage the growth of small plantations as a way round the increasing Communist influence among the working class of the large plantations.[69] A few attempts were made to reduce the numbers running away by providing garden plots, but such experiments had not become widespread before the outbreak of World War II. This form of working-class resistance to the conditions imposed upon them by the plantation owners therefore continued to be important.

When losses are taken in conjunction with the immigration and repatriation figures for the same years they give a picture of a highly unstable workforce. They also show why net reductions in the labour force began to occur in 1929 rather than 1931 (as was suggested by the data in Table 2.13).

From November 1928 the situation was exacerbated by the beginning of what the French termed a 'violent' propaganda campaign against contract labour recruitment launched by 'anti-French elements'. In February 1929 the director of a private recruitment agency was assassinated. It is to these events that the French attributed the decline in labour supply of the first half of 1929, prior to a precipitate fall of the rubber price.[70] In the second half of 1929 and the first half of 1930, there were four strikes at plantations in the south. At one of these, Phu Rieng in Bien Hoa province, police were used against the strikers, the leaders were imprisoned and the 'contaminated' workers were returned to their country of origin.[71] The strike had been organised by the newly formed Indo-Chinese Communist Party, as part of a campaign which culminated in the revolutionary movement of that year in the provinces of Ha Tinh and Nghe An.

But on the whole, the level of organisation of plantation workers was not high, and this is in part an attribute of and in part a factor contributing to the instability of the workforce. As it turned out, it was left up to the planters themselves and the French colonial authorities to enforce conditions on the plantations which would attract a more stable workforce. Although the French State clearly recognised that the discontent of the plantation labour force was provoked by the planters,[72] by 1937 it was clear that little had been done to rectify the situation.

In summary, then, we can say that in a period of expansion of the agricultural sector of southern Vietnam, with a high land–labour ratio which made local recruitment of labour for the plantations difficult, the transport of contract labour from northern and central Vietnam was vital to the expansion of rubber production as a major commodity export. However, aside from the effects of the international market, the conditions under which this contract labour lived and worked were deemed an important contributory factor to the instability of the plantation labour force and the programme was apparently based on a misconception as to the extent of labour surplus in the densely populated delta regions. These conclusions have significant implications for later efforts by the DRV government to reduce the overcrowding of the northern deltas and, in the post-1975 period, for the programme of restoring rubber production and opening up New Economic Zones. The keys to a successful programme of population movement would clearly lie both in a reduction of seasonal labour shortages in northern Vietnamese agriculture and in the ability to provide improved incentives and living conditions if the workforce was to have any commitment to the Zones.

CONCLUSION

The main areas of development of the Vietnamese economy during the French colonial period were in the export of primary commodities, the production and distribution of which was dominated by private French capital and concentrated in Cochin-China (except for mineral exports which were located in the north). Government investment in infrastructure, because it served the interests of capital, tended to reinforce this regional pattern of development. Although a limited transfer of economic surplus from Cochin-China to the rest of the country took place via the central budget mechanism, this was insufficient to bring about any fundamental alteration in the rate of growth of the more backward areas. Nor was the volume of trade between north and south large compared with intra-region or international trade. National economic integration thus remained at a low level.

I have not been able to find evidence to show that there was severe dislocation to the economy caused by the division of the country at the 17th parallel in 1954 and the complete cessation of economic contact in 1958. The potential for greater integration based on economic complementarity may indeed have existed prior to the First Indo-China War, but it was not yet an actuality. In the south, the rubber plantations were probably the worst affected, being cut off from a traditional source of labour supply, but they were in any case in a contested zone for most of the next two decades and this was probably a more important cause of their decline (as we shall see in the next chapter). The complaints, frequently voiced in the pre-war period, by southern businessmen over their disproportionate tax contribution to the central Government budget was dissipated. The period of unity under the French had little positive impact on northern development, other than that associated with development of certain primary exports. In my view, the shipment of large quantities of rice from south to north was less important than hitherto assumed – though the separation from this potential source may have been an added spur to the development of food self-sufficiency under the DRV.

However, the loss of the south could be regarded as a significant loss of a *potential* source of funds, and a potential market for mineral products. By forcing the north to begin the process of development without access to a part of the southern surpluses, the separation at Geneva ensured a greater reliance by the DRV on its own much more limited resources and correspondingly reduced the number of development policy options open to it – though of course this was partly offset by the availability of external resources from China and the Soviet Union. In the south, on the other hand, the attempt by the US to impose a political regime which had neither a broad political nor a broad economic base quickly led to civil conflict and caused the rapid dissipation of the economic surplus which had been the basis of Cochin-China's growth. This is the subject of the next chapter.

3 Economy of the Republic of Vietnam 1955–1975

This chapter and the next attempt to answer two questions: firstly, what were the major factors conditioning the development of the Southern Vietnamese economy between 1955 and 1975; secondly, what are the legacies of this development bequeathed to the new socialist regime, particularly those relevant to the question of unification?

In the present chapter I will explore the relationship between the changing social class structure of the Southern region during these two decades and the overall development of the economy. Chapter 4 narrows the focus to the rural sector. A discussion of the so-called 'Third Vietnam' – the area controlled by the National Liberation Front during the war – and its relationship to the economy of the RVN will also be left to Chapter 4 since it mainly concerns the rural areas. Indeed the analysis of the development of agriculture in the South cannot be separated from that concerning the social reforms carried out by the NLF in the zones it influenced.

The answer to the first question lies essentially in the social and political realm – in the backward class structure of Southern Vietnamese society left in the wake of the departing French and the intense political contradictions engendered by it. The outcome of these contradictions was a state of civil war, fuelled by the intervention of the United States, acting in the light of its own perceived interests of 'containing Communism' in South-East Asia. Escalation of the war throughout the 1960s in turn slowed both the transformation of the class structure and the productive diversification of the economy. Prior to 1970, US intervention served to shore up a regime which, because of the class interests it served, was unable to bring about an increased level of industrialisation. As we shall see in more detail in the next chapter, the efforts of the regime to halt and reverse the process of land reform taking place under Communist leadership, helped to repress agricultural growth. This in turn contributed to the failure of the manufacturing sector to expand.

The answer to the second question is a corollary of the first. In short, the lack of a coherent development strategy of the Southern regime and its political isolation from the bulk of the population (the peasantry) led to heavy reliance on economic and military aid from the United States to ensure its survival. A considerable increase in the commoditisation of the economy took place, based on this aid, particularly in the urban areas. However, the war reinforced a tendency among the wealthy to utilise aid for luxury consumption and investment in commercial enterprise rather than in productive capacity. The economy was characterised by negative savings throughout the period and the high levels of dependence on aid-financed imported consumer goods and inputs has had serious consequences for post-war development.

A third, related, issue which arises is that of how the recent economic history of Southern Vietnam affects the type of development strategy to the transition to a unified socialist economy. Some broad contours of a feasible development strategy emerge from a review of the 1955–75 period. These would appear to include the need to develop the southern agricultural sector by taking care with peasant incentives, the mobilisation of an economic surplus with greatly increased effectiveness of its utilisation and the minimisation of the political and economic strains imposed by open and hidden subsidies paid by the population of the North in order to sustain and develop the South (which in many respects, in per capita consumption for example, is already richer than the North).

The analysis of South Vietnamese economic development presented in this chapter differs in emphasis from the standard Marxist and radical analyses which tend to focus on American imperialism as the cause of the South's economic backwardness in this period (that is, the basic contradictions are seen as external to Vietnamese society rather than internal) and to treat the Diem/Thieu governments as 'puppet regimes'. This is not to deny the importance of the American intervention in South Vietnam, but to show that the American objective (of creating a viable capitalist state as a bulwark against Communism) was effectively frustrated, firstly, by the need to rely on a social group whose own aims were not entirely consistent with this objective and, secondly, by the active resistance of social groups organised under the Communist umbrella. American advisers consistently pressured President Ngo Dinh Diem to adopt more growth-orientated policies, but the latter was rather single-mindedly concerned with consolidating his domestic political power among the élite interest-groups of Southern society, making economic measures subservient to this end. At the same time, American dependence on Diem forced these advisers to ignore the fact that the fundamental causes of economic backwardness and communist insurgency lay in the system of land tenure which Diem was in the process of reinforcing.

The analysis presented here also differs from more orthodox interpretations, in focusing attention on this fundamental importance of the South Vietnamese class structure. The process of capitalist economic development presupposes a simultaneous transformation of the class structure, the development of an indigenous class of industrial capitalists and of an industrial proletariat. In South Vietnam, unlike South Korea, Taiwan and others, the degeneration into protracted civil war, sustained by escalating US intervention on behalf of its Vietnamese ally, hindered this transformation and tended to reinforce the dependence of the economy on external support.

SOCIAL STRUCTURE AND ECONOMIC GROWTH

As a result of the military successes of the Viet Minh against the French and the political settlement at Geneva in 1954, Vietnam was divided into two regroupment zones. Even in the southern part of the country, which was not ceded to the Communists, the Viet Minh had gained a substantial amount of political ground and there was widespread feeling in both Vietnam and the USA that, at the elections scheduled to be held in 1956, the Communists and their allies would win handsomely.[1] The United States Government, in its search for a reliable ally which would be capable of preventing a Communist victory in the South, was forced to turn to a social group which, far from having democratic credentials, was in fact more closely connected to Vietnam's feudal past – belonging to the old Mandarin landowning and bureaucratic strata – and had, in many cases, actively collaborated with the French colonial regime.

There was a very real sense in which the Ngo Dinh Diem Government, which was established in the South after the Geneva Conference, was a creation of the United States. Not only did Diem initially attain office as a result of US pressure on former emperor Bao Dai, he received active encouragement and assistance from US government departments and agencies in his policy of political repression carried out against political opponents (including the Viet Minh) and, in the assessment of US officials, could not have survived without that assistance.[2] The Diem regime was seen in Washington as an essential part of the strategy of containing Communism in South-East Asia.[3] Yet paradoxically, the social character of the regime in the context of deep-rooted popular and armed opposition meant that it also provided a major obstacle to the successful implementation of this strategy.

The success of the American initiatives towards Vietnam was predicated not only upon political repression of Communists and sympathisers, but also on the development and integration of South-East Asian economies into a wider emerging system of US-dominated production and trade.[4] South-East Asian countries were to provide raw materials and markets for American and Japanese manufacturing industry. Later on this role was extended to include certain aspects – mainly labour- and pollution-intensive ones – of the manufacturing process itself. In addition to its repressive anti-communist activities, the Diem regime was, therefore, expected by the Americans to establish a stable and growing capitalist economy which would provide its people with a rising standard of living and attract their support away from the Viet Minh.

The Diem government (1955–63) proved, however, that it was incapable of such an achievement within the timespan allotted to it. Although output growth was quite high during the period 1955–1960,[5] this can be partly ascribed to the effects of recovery from the devastation of both World War II and the subsequent anti-French resistance (the starting point was very low). The growth occurred in spite of very low rates of investment which would have been inadequate to sustain per capita income growth over the longer period (see page 58 for detailed discussion of this). However, much of the growth can be attributed to the effects of Viet Minh rent reductions and land reforms in stimulating increased agricultural productivity after peace was restored. Diem carried out his own land reform which was implemented gradually between 1956 and 1959 and which, in many instances, attempted to reverse the Viet Minh measures in order to return land to former landlords or create new ones from among the military officers loyal to him. It also exempted from redistribution any land under industrial crops or pasture – a way out for many landowners who were given twelve months to effect the conversion – and the ceiling on holdings of over 100 hectares was very high in any case (in Long An province, only 34 individuals owned more than the legal maximum, amounting to 10 per cent of the cultivated area).[6] Grievances over land distribution formed a major part of the Southern population's support for the Communists. The contrast here with the land reforms carried out in 1949 in Taiwan and South Korea is instructive. In these cases, reforms were carried out with the support of the peasantry and were successful in eliminating landlord influence in the economic sphere, thus removing an obstacle to rapid industrialisation.[7] Diem's 'reverse' reform placed something of a fetter on further agricultural growth, while at the same time, little effort was made to encourage investment in productive enterprises which might have led to more rapid growth of industry.[8]

A factor vexing the Americans was the regime's apparent preference for public rather than private enterprise (an idea similarly applied in other Asian states influenced by post-war nationalist ideas, as was the nationalisation of colonial estates) in an effort to encourage Vietnamese, as opposed to foreign and ethnic Chinese control over the economy. Musolf[9] gives ample evidence that such public control was essentially political in character and not primarily due to an attempt to influence the direction and pace of development, although it may well have been an essential pre-condition for the establishment of an indigenous industrial bourgeoisie. Later, the government tried to sell some of these public enterprises to wealthy Vietnamese. A more genuine bar to the growth of private enterprise was Diem's antagonisation of the ethnic Chinese business community, which might otherwise have been a key source of capital, through his attempts to force them to adopt Vietnamese nationality and adhere to Vietnamese law.

American worries continued after Diem's overthrow. In 1964, for example, US officials worried about Government efforts to control rice distribution centrally. This practice coincided with Vietnamese traditions under the monarchy. However, the US advisers would have preferred to stimulate rural production via fertilisers and seed programmes, relying on the market to ensure adequate distribution of agricultural surplus to urban consumers and for export.[10] Instead, successive South Vietnamese regimes saw centrally-controlled subsidised rice distribution as an important means of political control.

Diem's economic policies, together with an almost exclusive reliance on political repression as a means of defeating the opposition, resulted in his growing unpopularity among the people and consequent alarming (for the Government) successes for the National Front for the Liberation of South Vietnam (NLF) after 1960, when the Communist Party and its allies adopted the strategy of meeting the repression with armed struggle.[11] The political repression covered all opposition to Diem's family-based ruling group and, in 1963, provoked some leaders of South Vietnam's majority Buddhist religion to acts of self-immolation – events which met with violent retaliation against certain pagodas as centres of 'subversive' activity. This demonstrable inability of the Government to create either a broad political or economic base in the country greatly bothered its American advisers who ultimately colla-borated in Diem's overthrow in order to eliminate a client politician who had become an embarrassment.[12]

The explanations put forward by most Western economic observers for the failure of the South Vietnamese Government to get new investment started in the crucial period between the Geneva settlement and the beginning of escalation of the civil war in 1960 are based upon the stifling effect on enterprise of the many bureaucratic restrictions applying to persons wanting to establish a business[13] and the lack of a strong tradition of entrepreneurship in Vietnam (an explanation which tended to ignore the local Chinese). A recurring theme in these writings is, for example, the lack of a proper capital market.[14] Another hindrance to would-be private investors was seen in the practice of offering shares in denationalised companies within a fairly restricted circle: expropriated landlords holding Land Reform Bonds, the armed forces, civil servants and finally the general public, in that order.[15] In other words, ethnic Chinese businessmen tended to be low on the list of priorities, at least as long as the Diem regime lasted. While some of these explanations are undoubtedly important, they do not tell the whole story.

There is also a tendency in the literature on South Vietnam to attribute the alleged 'lack of entrepreneurial tradition' to cultural factors like Confucianism or the ideology of 'Personalism' of the Diem regime, which embody a number of features thought to be inimical to the rapid development of industrial enterprise. In so far as such explanations infer the absence of 'animal spirits', however, they must be regarded as wrong. In South Vietnam at the end of the First Indo-China War there was a sizeable entrepreneurial class, engaged chiefly in commercial activity. There was also a tiny group of indigenous owners of plantations[16] and some small scale, locally-owned manufacturing. Nor was this a recent phenomenon: it had existed through much of the colonial period and even earlier. Entrepreneurship was concentrated, however, overwhelmingly in commerce – not surprisingly, given the external orientation of the economy under the French. It was this concentration, rather than adherence to 'outmoded' ideologies which was the primary determinant of the entrepreneurial traditions and practices of the Vietnamese élite.

While the latter, including ethnic Chinese, had been largely confined to landowning, bureaucratic or commercial occupations, ownership of the so-called 'modern' sector of the economy (plantations, manufactur-ing industry) was, prior to 1955, almost entirely in French hands.[17]

With the departure of the French colonial power much of the productive capacity in the South nevertheless remained under French ownership[18] and there was no ready-made class of indigenous industrial entrepreneurs to step into its shoes.

French capital was concentrated in the plantation sector and in the services and infrastructure provided for them. The role of the plantations was as a supplier of raw materials to metropolitan French industry and as such they were not a dynamic element in the South Vietnamese economy. Not only were the supply and demand linkages primarily with France, but export earnings were scarcely reinvested in Vietnam itself and the Diem regime maintained excessively high international reserves instead of utilising them for development-oriented imports.[19] In contrast to the modern industrial sector of France which it served, the plantation sector of Vietnam was in fact 'backward', labour-intensive and relatively unskilled. The low wages of plantation workers had little multiplier effect. The same points can also be made about the other major export crops, rice and maize: the system of landownership and appropriation of farm surpluses as rent constituted institutional barriers to a deepening division of labour between agriculture and industry. On the one hand, peasant incomes were squeezed by demands for rent usually in excess of 50 per cent of the crop in government-controlled areas, reducing their demand for manufactured goods. On the other, the accumulation of wealth by Vietnamese landlords, for reasons which will become apparent later, tended not to lead to the creation of new productive capacity and employment. Instead, the rising wealth of the South Vietnamese élite was manifested in a housing and real estate boom in Saigon, rising black market prices of gold and foreign exchange and increased consumption of luxury goods like limousines, hi-fi sets, water skis, etc.[20]

After the initial post-war reconstruction phase of 1955–9 the growth which took place was, I shall argue, strongly related to the success of the NLF in breaking the grip of landlords in the countryside. In the urban areas, growth of the service sector was increasingly financed by American aid, although much potential growth (via diversification of production into manufacturing, for example) continued to be dissipated in luxury consumption. The tendency towards commoditisation of the rural economy (though very much interrupted by escalating warfare between 1965 and 1968 in particular) therefore depended on a growing quantity of US aid-financed imports rather than extension of the division of labour between agriculture and domestic industry.

The early period after the Geneva settlement had been an optimistic one, from the point of view of both the United States and its South Vietnamese allies: a combination of American largesse, and progress before 1959 in destroying the remaining Viet Minh infrastructure in the South, seemed to suggest that both economic development and consolidation of an anti-communist regime would become possible. However, the contradictions already apparent in Vietnamese society meant that in the 1960s the situation would become more difficult to manage. On the one hand, because of the lack of real support for the American-backed regime, especially in the rural areas, the leaders who replaced Diem necessarily came from the same social strata as their predecessor.[21] These political figures and officials were, on the whole, content to continue the policy of relying on massive American economic aid plus inflationary deficit-financing to maintain and improve the incomes and living standards of the urban population. A very high proportion of investment continued to be channelled into the foreign trade sector, particularly into lucrative importing businesses – a process encouraged by the maintenance of an over-valued exchange rate. The preference of investors for the commercial sector also provided cover for capital flights through over-inventory of imports, with excess foreign exchange deposited in the importer's account at an overseas bank. French plantation owners used this method too.[22] While high levels of imports were generally viewed as a means of restraining inflationary pressures, profiteering in the import trade was also cited as an important cause of inflation.[23] Corruption was endemic to a system in which successive military dictators used access to the American aid-financed consumer bonanza as a means of tightening their political control. It was only the setbacks of the 1968 Tet Offensive and impending American withdrawal from the arena in the 1970s which forced the government of President Thieu to adopt a different strategy.

These events revealed the full extent of the RVN regime's weakness and compelled it to take a more active hand in bringing about the conditions for economic development. From 1970 the regime instituted a four-pronged programme: the 'Land-to-the-Tiller' reform,[24] a foreign investment policy designed to encourage and facilitate foreign investment, a 'green revolution' in agriculture and an investment policy which gave priority to projects which would help the Republic to overcome its enormous balance of payments deficit (by reducing imports, expanding exports, using local raw materials in industry).[25]

The results of these policies are difficult to assess. There had been a tendency for the output–capital ratio to rise between 1966 and 1970 (the ratio of GDP to gross capital formation rose from an average of 1.1 in 1961–5 to 2.4 in 1966–70 and fell to 1.6 in 1971–2 on the basis of data given in the Appendix to this chapter). However, it is not clear that the growth in incomes related to new capital investment had occurred as a result of an increased division of labour between (and rising labour productivity in) agriculture and industry.[26] The fact that, after 1970, the Government tried to change the direction of investment by the above-mentioned policies, suggests that it had not. On top of this, the Thieu regime was unable to bring about the restraint in the rate of consumption out of national income which would have been needed in order to raise the rate of savings and investment. Although calls were made by the Government for voluntary consumer spending restraint[27] and heavy duties were imposed on luxury items, the regime was politically unable effectively to tax either the wealthy classes upon whom it depended for support or the peasantry over whose allegiance it vied with the NLF.

By the mid-1960s the hopes of achieving economic development comparable to that then beginning to appear in Taiwan and South Korea were, at best, put in abeyance by the escalation of war. The importance of this for the course of both economic growth and class formation should not be underestimated. In particular, considerable destruction of the rural sectors of the economy occurred, leading to a big decline in rubber production and to stagnation in rice output.[28] Prior to the war those two crops provided the major portion of South Vietnam's export income,[29] so subsequent decline contributed substantially to heavy reliance on American aid to finance the current account-deficit as well as reducing the availability of domestically produced surpluses for investment and consumption purposes. Hence the war itself was a major factor in the failure of the South Vietnamese élite to develop its economic activities beyond commercial capital into productive capacity (as had their counterparts in, for example, Taiwan, South Korea and Singapore).

Inaccessibility and/or insecurity of the rural areas, however, cannot wholly account for this failure. Wars can provide a stimulus to production in areas not directly affected – a condition which applied to the cities of South Vietnam, except briefly during the 1968 Tet Offensive – so some other explanation must be found for the lack of progress in industrialisation, especially of the export-orientated variety.

Two other reasons which have been put forward for the poor medium-term growth of the Southern economy are related to the effects of the war: first, the diversion of manpower into defence-related activities and, second, the adverse impact of inflationary financing of the war effort.

The problem of manpower diversion is treated below (see section on employment, page 76) where it is argued that the evidence for its impact on the economy is ambiguous.

The inflationary impact of deficit financing is of some importance. Domestic revenue collection covered a relatively small proportion of government expenditure, on account of the difficulty for the regime of directly taxing either the peasantry or the Saigon middle and upper classes, upon whom it depended for its legitimacy.[30] Over half the tax revenues were derived from various imposts on the (largely US financed) import trade.[31] US aid Counterpart Funds accounted, on average, for almost 30 per cent of total revenue, but the domestic deficit (after taking aid revenue into account) still remained high at over 28 per cent of government expenditure.[32] This portion was financed either by National Bank 'advances' to the Treasury (that is, printing money), or sales of local currency to US personnel and creation of US dollar reserves.[33] Thus the contribution of the US to the budget support of the Republic of Vietnam was very high, both *directly* through aid and piastre purchases and *indirectly* through taxes on US aid-financed imports. Chi Do Pham estimated that the US financial prop covered 43 per cent of South Vietnamese Government expenditure between 1960 and 1965 and 49 per cent from 1965 to 1972.[34] These figures do not include US military aid.

In the absence of government borrowing from the public, methods of deficit financing involved increases in the money supply and added inflationary pressures to the economy. Inflation does seem, however, to have been held below the rates of money-supply increase, mainly because of the Commercial Import Program.[35]

The high rates of inflation which prevailed in South Vietnam throughout the period undoubtedly contributed to 'resource misallocation', in particular by the encouragement of short-term speculative investments rather than productive ones. But it is also necessary to look at the nature of the government expenditure and the essentially *political* reasons for the large deficits. Defence took 57 per cent of government expenditure in 1960–74.[36] Other important items of budgetary expenditure were subsidies on rice and to public enterprises aimed at keeping down prices of goods and services produced by them.[37] This was part of a package, along with the high wages and salaries paid to all government employees, to encourage continued loyalty to the Government and to reduce corruption.[38] For the most part, such efforts did not succeed. Real wages of government employees, including soldiers, tended to fall over time, leading to a vicious cycle of corruption and looting by troops. In the long run the depredations of ARVN soldiers were an important reason for the collapse of the regime and continuing popular support for the revolutionaries.

US aid levels were decided on the basis of expected imports (minus foreign-exchange reserves). This encouraged the Government to maintain an overvalued piastre, in order to sustain high levels of import demand, as did the inelasticity of US troop demand for local currency. US aid policy thus reinforced the dependence of the regime on imported goods, and short-term political contingencies ensured that the policy could not be changed. The possibility of either import-substituting or export-led industrialisation was therefore correspondingly inhibited. This constitutes an important difference with the South Korean and Taiwanese 'models' in which currency devaluations in the early 1960s provided a stimulus to industrial growth.

High levels of government expenditure coupled with inability to increase domestic revenue sources were, therefore, structural concomitants of the political and class basis of the regime – its lack of a firm base of support among the peasantry, its inability to sustain itself in power without extensive US aid and use of military force, its strategy of winning the 'hearts and minds' of the people through provision of imported consumer goods, and its pursuit of policies which created obstacles to transforming that productive capacity in the long run.

These points have important consequences for the study of post-1975 problems of transition because they highlight the extreme dependence of South Vietnam upon American aid for the maintenance of living standards of the population and the severe problems brought about by the cessation of this aid in keeping political stability and generating sources of finance for investment. The extent of this dependence is examined below.

It should be emphasised that it has not been my intention in this section to argue that the South Vietnamese regime was totally incapable of bringing about a transformation in the long term. Some industrialisation did begin under the Diem regime, especially through the establishment of public enterprise in cement, textiles, paper, sugar refining, agricultural machinery,[39] as well as a number of private enterprises in textiles and food processing (although in many cases to the detriment of competing handicraft-producers). But the stimulus to growth of industry depended in large measure on rising peasant demand for consumer goods and manufactured inputs. As we shall see, this in turn depended upon successful land reform and the transfer of agricultural surpluses from landlords to peasants. It was not until the 1970s when, it could be argued, the war was already lost, that the South Vietnamese regime ceased to offer strong resistance to the peasant pressure for such reforms. The availability of generous quantities of external resources might also have encouraged productive diversification of the economy in the longer term, but in the short term (as in many other developing countries, including the Philippines under Marcos) it served as a disincentive to productive investment. Extreme pressure on the regime from the National Liberation Front and the necessity to preserve existing bases of support prevented the undertaking of policies designed to increase import-substitution and exports.

An example of the view of American experts on the causes of the poor economic development performance, one that stresses quantitative rather than qualitative factors, was put by F. C. Child, a member of the Michigan State University Advisory Group on Vietnam. His analysis is worth discussing here because it contains a number of common oversimplifications and it shows how a misunderstanding of the nature of the development process under capitalism could lead to dire warnings for the future that were basically ill-founded.

Child argued that the basic problem was the poor *rate* of investment: he estimated that in 1955, 1956 and 1960 net investment was only two to five per cent of the net national product of South Vietnam.[40] He suggested that although reasonably high growth rates were achieved in the period up to 1960, these were due chiefly to the return of the population to productive activity in the aftermath of the French War and the investment rate remained insufficient for capital formation to sustain growth. Given an expected population growth rate of three per cent per annum, Child estimated that a nine per cent rate of new capital formation would be required to maintain per capita income at existing levels.[41] He pointed out that since 1955 most aid received from the United States had been used for consumption purposes, also that very large foreign exchange reserves were invested in Western banks instead of being used productively inside Vietnam.[42] Unless something was done to raise the investment rate, these funds would later have to be used to sustain consumption levels of the growing population. Since with a given incremental capital–output ratio, the rate of growth of the economy is dependent upon the rate of investment (savings in Child's model), a declining rate of gross investment would mean an ever larger proportion of the total taken up by depreciation of old capital stock, a declining share of new investment and an accelerating decline in the growth of the economy.[43] Child predicted that if the then current trend continued, net capital formation would cease in 1967.

The argument was over-simple because it ignored possible improvements in the capital–output ratio and there was also the problem that the population growth rate might warrant a higher investment rate than was attainable. Compression of consumption to achieve a high rate of investment can have a detrimental effect on labour productivity and ultimately lead to reduced levels of output and investible surplus. In fact growth continued to be respectable in South Vietnam during the early 1960s in spite of continued low rates of net investment (see further on pages 63 and 89).

Child also failed to understand that the process of transforming a commercially orientated economy into an industrial one involves not only a certain amount of investment in productive capacity, but also the transformation of a class of commercial capitalists into one of industrial capitalists. Accumulation of capital through trade does not automatically lead to the development of modern industry. Before this can happen, the conditions must be created under which entrepreneurs will find it more lucrative to invest in industry (and agriculture) rather than in more traditional avenues. Vietnamese capital, in the colonial and immediate post-colonial period, was heavily concentrated in landownership and commerce. The problem facing advocates of industrialisation, therefore, was not of the rate of investment alone: it was also a question of creating the necessary and sufficient conditions for investment (including foreign investment) to be pushed or pulled into industry (that is, by making land and commerce relatively less attractive).

In South Korea and Taiwan, two models often held up for Vietnamese emulation, this process of class transformation took more than a decade after World War II before it began to produce rapid industrial growth rates in the 1960s.[44] South Vietnam in the 1950s pursued many of the same policies as the American-backed government of these two countries (nationalising the property of the former colonial power, land reform, establishing public enterprises in key sectors, creating infrastructure financed by American aid). There were, however, crucial differences. In Taiwan, for example, the Chinese capitalists who fled there in 1949 already had a substantial background in industry. South Vietnam's initial land reform, in 1956, was carried out in direct opposition to a more popular Communist-inspired reform. The economic returns to landownership remained high in areas under control of the South Vietnamese Government, but growth of the rural insurgency did have a similar effect to the land reforms of South Korea and Taiwan in reducing the desirability of landownership as an avenue of investment.[45] On the other hand, even for landlords thus affected, the greater uncertainty under conditions of escalating warfare (South Korea's war was much shorter) were not conducive to productive investment – particularly outside the cities. Hence the twin effects of an inadequate land reform and escalation of war hindered very much the formation of an industrial capitalist class in South Vietnam and helped prevent the very growth which was the American objective.

THE PATTERN OF GROWTH AND STAGNATION

The pattern of growth and stagnation which took place in the South Vietnamese economy as a result of these factors during the 1960s and seventies had important legacies for the Communist regime after 1975 since the productive capacity and structural problems it produced constituted the raw material from which a unified economy had to be built.

Data on national income growth and domestic capital formation after 1960 are unfortunately not directly comparable with those used by Child. While statistics on Gross Domestic Product and Gross Domestic Capital Formation are available, estimates of net capital formation can only be obtained for 1961–70. Gross capital formation data can have advantages over net investment figures because of the embodiment of new techniques in replacement capital,[46] but this observation may be of dubious value in the case of Vietnam because of the rather high proportion of replacement capital that is likely to have been taken up by restoration of infrastructure and productive capacity in the rural areas most affected by the war. There is no information on stock accumulation. In calculating per capita growth rates I have found that Child's estimate of the population growth rate (at about 3 per cent) is more useful than some more recent Vietnamese data based on an assumed growth rate of 2.6 per cent.[47]

There remains the problem of the measure of real rates of growth. The South Vietnamese economy suffered from variable but high rates of inflation throughout the period and some attempt has to be made to eliminate the effects of this from the analysis if we are to obtain any idea of the real growth of the economy. The only available figures are in 1960 constant prices which introduce distortions on account of different rates of price change for various commodities and services where weight in total product varies. It will be necessary at a later stage, then, to look at the sectors of the economy in more detail in order to substantiate the conclusions reached below.

Bearing these qualifications in mind, it is nevertheless possible to discern some general features of the pattern of investment and growth in South Vietnam during the two decades under consideration. The data shown in Appendix 3.1 suggest an average annual growth rate of real GDP of 3.4 per cent. However, three distinct periods are observable: the first, from 1955–61 shows an average growth rate of real GDP of 4 per cent per annum; the second, from 1961–68, 3.9 per cent, and the third, from 1968–74, a rate of 2.2 per cent. These figures indicate a tendency towards stagnation and decline of *per capita* GDP over the period. There also appear to be cyclical movements of the economy corresponding roughly to this periodisation (see Figure 3.1). The first period of growth is the period of recovery from war and ends in 1961, coinciding with a poor harvest which may also be related to the escalation of armed struggle by the NLF. The second period ends with the destruction caused by fighting during the 1968 Tet Offensive. Growth in this period was especially rapid during 1962–5 and can

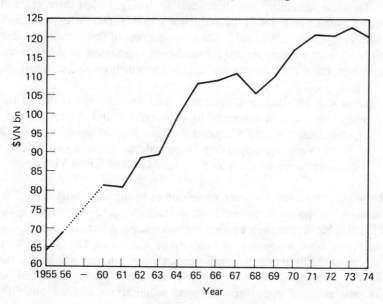

Figure 3.1   South Vietnam: GDP at constant 1960 prices
Source: Appendix 3.1.

probably be attributed to two major causes: on the one hand, rent reductions and redistribution of land by the NLF leaving farm surpluses in the hands of peasants, and on the other hand, increasing economic involvement by the US in the form of the Commercial Import Program.[48] The good growth rate of the economy certainly occurred despite continued deterioration of government security in the countryside.[49]

In spite of rising levels of commodity aid, the escalation of American military involvement was accompanied by rapid inflation in 1966 and relative stagnation in the real growth rate of the economy during 1966–67.[50] In 1968 a big drop in production was recorded as a result of damage caused by the Tet Offensive (another major offensive by the Communists at Easter 1972 was probably the cause of another dip in production figures for that year) and the rapid growth of the years 1969–71 was at least partly due to restoration of productive capacity. US commodity-aid levels also reached their peak during this period. However, the main factor behind this phase of growth is probably the reduced level of fighting as both sides recovered from the losses of 1968 and peace negotiations were begun in Paris. This was a key period of sustained growth in rice production (Figure 3.3a).

The clear tendency towards stagnation during the last three years of the Republic is a result of reductions in US piastre expenditures following troop withdrawal.[51] The consequences of this withdrawal and the cutting of US military aid for the South Vietnamese economy were, however, more than merely cyclical. In the words of Arthur Smithies,

> when it is recalled that equipment and ammunition is not in the budget at all, and amounts to between 2.5 and 3 times budget expenditures, it is simply beyond the bounds of imagination to think of South Vietnam supporting its own defence. Total expenditures could amount to as much as the whole GNP of South Vietnam.[52]

In other words, the diversion of resources to the war effort needed to sustain the political power of the regime would have had quite catastrophic consequences for the economic structure. Moreover, economic and budgetary difficulties of these last few years were accompanied by rising demoralisation, corruption and plunder by the RVN's badly paid troops and civil servants. These combined to increase political opposition from all social strata and undoubtedly were a major factor in hastening its demise.

At first glance, American efforts to encourage an increase in capital formation would appear to have borne fruit soon after the assassination of Diem. Net investment rose to seven per cent of GDP in 1964 and to nearly 12 per cent in 1966 before beginning to tail off again subsequently (see Appendix, page 89). There are some less satisfactory aspects of this, however. In the years of relative stagnation in real output growth of 1966–7, for example, the investment rate was sustained at high levels, causing a sharp rise in investment–output ratios. Given that these were also years of great uncertainty because of both rapid inflation and concern for the future safety of the Republic, it is likely that a high proportion of this investment comprised accumulation of inventories. Moreover, it is a corollary of the primarily *commercial* orientation of the South Vietnamese capitalists, reinforced by the nature of the war economy, the free availability of large quantities of United States aid and the foreign exchange allocation system, that a high proportion of investment was in any case directed towards the requirements of importing enterprises rather than towards creation of productive capacity for the domestic and export markets. Nothing more definite can be said about sectoral composition of investment or its breakdown into fixed assets and stocks, in the absence of additional data.

There is further indirect evidence to suggest that the main factors holding back growth of the economy were social and political rather than quantitative lack of investment or physical war damage. Firstly, the years 1969–73 were relatively good years for the Republic of Vietnam from a 'security' point of view. The National Liberation Front had suffered very heavy losses during the Tet Offensive, so that the considerable gains made during the early 1960s could no longer be sustained while government forces were able to recover more quickly and occupy a number of areas previously held or disputed by the Front.[53] Moreover, it was in the manufacturing sector which was heavily concentrated in certain enclaves, particularly around the Saigon and Bien Hoa area, and was therefore far more secure from NLF activity than the rest of the country, that some of the heaviest cutbacks in growth took place (Figure 3.2).[54]

Secondly, estimates can be obtained of the value of output in the six 'productive' sectors of the economy (agriculture, mining, manufacturing, construction, transport, public utilities) and in the services sector – again using 1960 constant prices.[55] These figures show that the share of the six sectors tended to decline markedly over the 14 years from 1960. Their combined average real growth rate was only 1.4 per cent, compared with an overall real GDP growth rate of 2.8 per cent. From

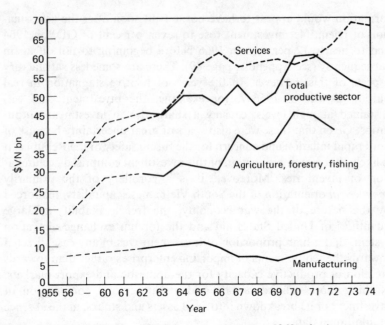

Figure 3.2   South Vietnam: GDP by sector (constant 1960 prices)
Source: Tinh Hinh Kinh Te Mien Nam 1955–75 (Ho Chi Minh City, 1979)
pp. 116–18.

1960 to 1967, the growth rate of the six 'productive' sectors was 3.1 per
cent compared with 4.4 per cent for total GDP, but after 1967, growth
of the former group was eliminated altogether (−0.3 per cent per
annum). The service sector (including banking and insurance, commerce, administration and defence, property and real estate and
miscellaneous services), on the other hand, showed an annual growth
rate for the whole period of 4.1 per cent.

Figure 3.2 brings into relief the contrasting performance of these two
areas of the economy. In fact outside the above-delineated 'services'
sector, only agriculture, forestry and fishing showed a marked increase
in real value of output after 1960. While this is an important exception,
since it produced an estimated one-third of GDP, the stagnation of
manufacturing is also highly significant because of its great potential
for dynamism. Commerce grew by two and a half times between 1960
and 1962 and nearly doubled its share of GDP, while banking and
insurance more than doubled its share and trebled in size. The
administration and defence sector doubled in size with the escalation of

war in the early 1960s (growing from 16 to 24 per cent of GDP), but appears to have stabilised after that. The growth of the banking and commercial sectors, on the other hand, had a common basis in the expansion of imports financed by American aid. The greater proportion of lending by the private banks of South Vietnam was for financing the export-import trade.[56] These two sectors provided a safe avenue for investment by the South Vietnamese capitalists.

In fact the United States, while urging more investment in agriculture and industry upon successive governments of South Vietnam, in practice encouraged the growth of short-term commercial investments, often *at the expense* of the development of production. The primary cause of this paradox was that short-term political contingencies usually dictated US aid-distribution and Vietnamese use of that aid.[57] The pattern of American aid was also influenced by American domestic interests, particularly US rice-growers, to make South Vietnam increasingly dependent upon imported, rather than domestically produced foodstuffs. The Asian Development Bank reported that Public Law 480 rice shipments were used in Vietnam to subsidise US rice production, transforming the US into the world's largest rice-exporting country, and suggested that this may have discouraged efforts to keep the NLF from controlling the Mekong delta.[58] The Thai government also expressed concern at loss of rice sales to Vietnam due to American surplus rice exports under PL 480 arrangements.[59] These factors probably succeeded in keeping the rate of increase of rice prices within South Vietnam below the general rate of inflation, giving a disincentive to farmers. Increases in the Saigon rice price averaged only 27 per cent per annum between 1965 and 1971, compared with a rise of 34 per cent per annum in the consumer price index for the Saigon working class.[60]

SECTORAL CONTRIBUTIONS TO GROWTH

During 1960–74 more than half the workforce of South Vietnam was in farming and about 30–40 per cent of output value was produced by this sector. Manufacturing declined from 11 per cent of the total GDP in 1960 to 6.5 per cent in 1972, while services increased their share from 48 to 52 per cent.[61]

The preponderance of agriculture within the productive sector and its central importance in the process of North–South integration warrant a separate chapter. What follows here is, therefore, only a preliminary survey of the main developments in output.

In so far as it is possible to ascertain in the development of agricultural production, given the obvious pitfalls in using data from the less secure areas, it would appear that, with some notable exceptions, ouput tended to stagnate during the 1960s and 1970s (Figures 3.3 a–d). This tendency is brought out more sharply by figures on per capita production of the most important crop, paddy (Table 3.1). Agriculture was undoubtedly the sector most directly affected by war damage. In many areas, whole villages and their fields were abandoned by peasants fleeing war-ravaged zones; others were rendered infertile by defoliation, intensive bombing, etc. As the war spread during the 1960s, these factors are reflected in declining or stagnant production figures which do not begin to recover, in most cases, until 1973, the year of the Paris Peace Agreement. Rubber production, which was concentrated in the war-torn highlands also fell dramatically, even though the area under cultivation increased,[62] due to lack of investment or replanting programmes and disruption of transport to and from the main areas.[63] Given rubber's prominent position in South Vietnam's export profile,[64] the impact on the balance of trade was such that exports came to count little towards the balance of payments. Sugar production also fell after 1965 and from that time 90 per cent of the raw sugar for the South Vietnamese mills was imported.[65]

Rice production, after expanding in the 1950s and early sixties, began to decline in 1964, leading to the drying-up of Vietnam's exportable surplus, although output began to recover in the 1970s. After 1964, South Vietnam became a large-scale net importer of rice.[66] As has been noted above, some accounts charge that it was deliberate policy of the United States, aimed at promoting American rice production, that led, directly or indirectly, to the neglect of investment in the crucial Mekong delta area. South Vietnam certainly absorbed a very high share of US rice exports and a positive relationship can be found between its capacity to absorb these exports and the expansion of American rice production.[67] However, there was considerable improvement in South Vietnamese rice production in the early 1970s, possibly due to improved security of tenure under the new land reform, eleventh-hour application of 'green revolution' techniques and declining levels of fighting in the delta as the war switched from its guerrilla phase to one of more conventional warfare centred in the less agriculturally important areas. The implication is that while US policy of promoting American rice exports failed positively to encourage investment in agricultural production, it was rather the combined effects of war and the resistance of the South Vietnamese regime itself to a much

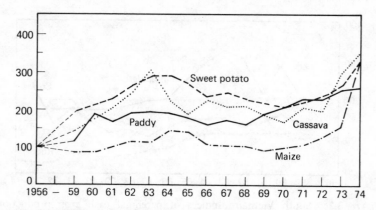

Figure 3.3a   South Vietnam: Indices of staple grain production (1956 = 100)
Source: Tinh Hinh Kinh Te Mien Nam 1955–75, pp. 136, 139–40.

needed land reform until too late in the day which had brought about the earlier stagnation of production.[68] Once the reform had been carried out the threat of war had receded and, crucially, a ready supply of consumer goods and modern inputs became available to the peasants via the Commercial Import Program (CIP); output began to expand rapidly.

Nevertheless, the problem of feeding a swollen urban population

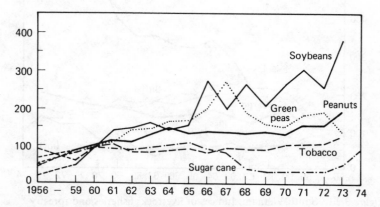

Figure 3.3b   South Vietnam: Indices of annual cash crop production (1960 = 100)
Source: Tinh Hinh Kinh Te Mien Nam 1955–75, pp. 139–40.

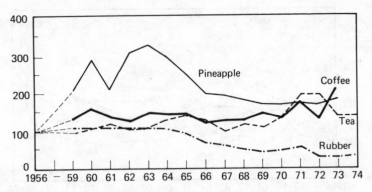

Figure 3.3c   South Vietnam: Indices of perennial cash crop production (1956 = 100)
Source: Tinh Hinh Kinh Te Mien Nam 1955–75, pp. 138–40.

once the Americans withdrew their supply was a serious one, particularly in view of the fact that neither the Diem or Thieu governments had tried seriously to implement taxation of the peasants.[69] Getting enough surplus agricultural product into the towns and to the rice-

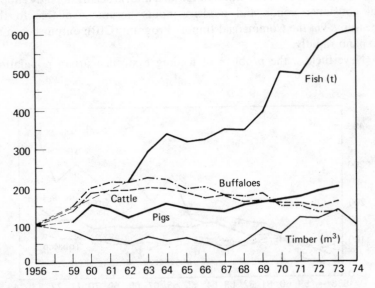

Figure 3.3d   South Vietnam: Indices of livestock, fisheries and forestry production (1956 = 100)
Source: Tinh Hinh Kinh Te Mien Nam 1955–75, pp. 140, 142.

Table 3.1   Per capita paddy production 1956–74 (kg)

1956	217	1960	346	1965	289	1970	292
1957	245	1961	313	1966	251	1971	313
1958	298	1962	342	1967	263	1972	304
1959	234	1963	339	1968	237	1973	327
		1964	320	1969	269	1974	321

Source   Calculated from paddy output figures in *THKTMN*, p. 136. Population series has been calculated on the basis of an estimate of 12.6 m. in 1956 (ibid., p. 215) and the 1976 census figure of 23.3 m. (Tong Cuc Thong Ke, *So Lieu Thong Ke 1930–1984*, Hanoi, 1985, p. 14) giving a population growth rate of 3.2% p.a.

deficit areas of northern and central Vietnam has proved a major problem both during the war and in later years.[70] The stagnation of rice production thus introduced a qualitatively new factor into Vietnamese economic life, with serious ramifications for future policy. The availability of a paddy surplus in the South could no longer be taken for granted.

Some other crops showing substantial improvements in output during the last few years of the regime, usually for the same reasons that paddy output increased, were secondary foodgrains (maize, sweet potato, cassava), pig-raising and cash crops like groundnuts, tobacco, coffee and tea. The production of timber also made considerable strides in the 1970s – possibly due to attempts to expand export income and increase the use of local raw materials in industry[71] (though this was accompanied by declining output of firewood and charcoal so that locally available fuels had to be replaced by imported ones).[72] One important exception to the general pattern of farm production over the period was soybeans which showed a more persistent tendency towards expansion. The fishing industry also underwent a sustained boom, especially towards the end of the regime, and both fishing and fish processing look to be very promising export areas.[73] Fisheries, perhaps because of their distance from the fighting, received some foreign investment (see Table 3.4) which may help to explain the growth in this area.

The apparent discrepancy between data on physical production levels and the much better performance of agriculture, forestry and fishing recorded in the data on real GDP can be partly explained by the expansion in the above areas of high unit value products. But it is difficult, on the basis of the data available, to explain the apparent recovery of growth in value of agricultural output as early as 1967 at a time when most crops were at low levels of production. It is possible that the effects of inflation have not been completely eliminated from the real GDP figures, but it is also possible that the discrepancy is due to unreliability of data collected by understaffed departments, working under difficult conditions and influenced by corruption. However, the trends are sufficiently marked for the figures to be useful as a rough guide.

The share of industrial production in GDP was always small and shrank rapidly after 1971. The sector was also highly concentrated, both geographically and in terms of the proportion of total output produced by a small number of firms. According to Moody,[74] 80 per cent of the membership of the Vietnam Confederation of Industry and Handicrafts (CADIA) were based in the Saigon/Gia Dinh/Bien Hoa area and only 9 sizeable factories (both CADIA and non-CADIA) operated outside this area. Two breweries (both French-owned, and established prior to 1954) produced 99 per cent of output in beverages, by far the most important industry. In the tobacco industry, the second largest, two more French firms produced all of the legal output.[75] Other key industries which were also highly concentrated were food-processing, textiles and chemical products (pharmaceuticals). Seven firms produced 97 per cent of output in food-processing; in textile manufacturing 24 firms produced 97 per cent and in pharmaceuticals, 20 firms produced 92 per cent.[76] These few firms employed 99 per cent (beverages), 100 per cent (tobacco), 79 per cent (food-processing), 69 per cent (textiles) and 76 per cent (pharmaceuticals) of the workforce in their respective branches, yet represented only a small percentage of the firms operating in each industry.[77]

Since these five industries together represented 70 to 90 per cent of total industrial output in the late 1960s,[78] it seems important to assess their actual and potential contribution to economic growth. In each of the five industries, however, the record was not very impressive. All were heavily dependent upon imported raw materials, the share of imports in raw materials for 1968 (the only year for which there are data) being: beverages 85 per cent; tobacco 95 per cent; food-processing 70 per cent; textiles 95 per cent; pharmaceuticals 90 per cent.[79] Yet these are nearly all industries which should have considerable supply linkages to domestic primary production. Uncertainty in obtaining supplies from the war-torn countryside (especially in 1968) will be part of the explanation for this, but the obverse side of the coin is the ease of obtaining imports via the US aid programme.

It has already been noted that manufacturing was one of the sectors of the economy in which real GDP stagnated or declined between 1960 and 1974. An alternative picture of developments in three out of the five major branches mentioned above can be obtained by looking at production volumes (Figure 3.4a). Figure 3.4b shows the situation of some other industries for which data are available. South Vietnamese manufacturing catered almost entirely for the domestic market and these figures once again emphasise the importance of American piastre expenditures inside the country for stimulating the growth of industrial production, especially during 1965–7 and 1969–71. Rapid decline of output in nearly all branches followed American troop withdrawal. This American presence was also highly important for determining the structure of industrial production – the extraordinarily high proportions of manufacturing output accounted for by beer and tobacco can be seen in Table 3.2. Note, however, that for the main branches, nearly all the large firms were already operating prior to 1963.[80] Development during the subsequent period appears to have reinforced existing biases in the industrial structure. Major developments were geared to meet the consumption needs of the occupying forces (French or American) and wealthy Saigonese. There was relatively little development of manufacturing for export or to meet the demand of peasants (apart from a few shops assembling small farm machines from imported components). The lack of either export-orientation (discouraged by the over-valued

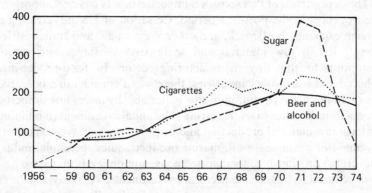

Figure 3.4a   South Vietnam: Index of consumer goods output (1963 = 100)
Source: Tinh Hinh Kinh Te Mien Nam 1955–75, pp. 171–2.

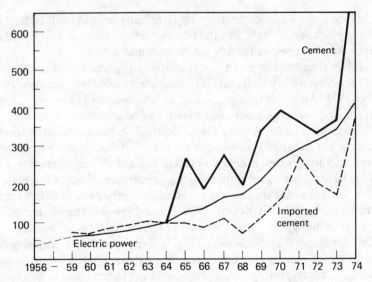

Figure 3.4b   South Vietnam: Index of producer goods output (1964 = 100)
Source: Tinh Hinh Kinh Te Mien Nam 1955–75, pp. 171–2.

exchange rate) or a significant ability of industry to provide inputs and consumer goods to peasants was a function of the regime's reliance on American commodity-aid to purchase political compliance, placing a further obstacle in the path of the US objective of creating a viable capitalist development process which could effectively defuse the Communist 'threat'.

The dependence of this sector on imported inputs has had important consequences in the post-war period. Cessation of US aid, creating a foreign exchange bottleneck, and other Western aid and trade restrictions,[81] led to raw material and spare-parts shortages and severe disruption to this tiny manufacturing sector. In food-processing, tobacco and some other industries, there was a considerable potential for rapid import substitution of raw materials[82] by increasing domestic production. In other cases, requiring substantial investment in building up local raw material production and/or providing an increased export revenue (for example, in oil, marine products, silica, perennial industrial crops) previously aid-supported consumption levels may have had to be reduced to finance the necessary investments. This may also have been a problem where re-tooling was needed to handle raw materials of a different quality from the previously imported ones or if spare parts

Table 3.2   Distribution of manufacturing output by Industry (%)

Industry	1962	1970*	1970†
Food processing	15.5	9.3	10.0
Beverages	48.2	59.1	30.0
Tobacco	14.6	13.3	13.0
Textiles	11.5	9.2	9.0
Chemical products	2.0	1.8	8.0
Total	91.8	92.7	70.0

*Derived from figures in National Institute of
Statistics, *Statistical Yearbooks*; † Figures given to
Moody by National Bank officials.
Source   Dale L. Moody, *The Manufacturing Sector
in the Republic of Vietnam*, University of Florida,
PhD thesis, 1975, pp. 89–90.

for the foreign machinery were unavailable. The extent of the reduction would be dependent on such factors as capital–output ratios, gestation lags, the ability to mobilise labour, access to other sources of foreign aid or aid from the North, so absence of attention to this problem by post-war planners could greatly exacerbate difficulties to the population caused by these bottlenecks.

Other substantial bottlenecks existed under (or as a result of) the wartime regime. The construction industry, for example – after an initial boom – was heavily affected by the war, leaving an acute shortage of housing for the swollen urban populations as well as shortages of all other kinds of buildings.[83] Moreover, domestic cement production was unable to meet more than 35 per cent of total requirements at the most.[84]

Much of the American development effort went into the building of infrastructure, chiefly for war purposes. This resulted in the appearance of a network of good roads – even super-highways on some of the more heavily-used routes such as that from Saigon to Bien Hoa – and led to rapid growth of the number of cars and trucks in the country.[85] By the 1970s, road transport was the main means of transport for non-military goods. Although air transport and coastal shipping were also available, the former was often unreliable because of shortages of space due to military priority[86] and the latter was subject to congestion in South Vietnam's few sizeable ports.[87] Road transport was considered the most reliable, presumably because drivers were able to get through by paying taxes (and bribes) to both RVN government and NLF officials *en route*.[88]

The consequences of this development have been two-edged. On the one hand it meant that South Vietnam came to rely heavily upon imported inputs – both vehicles and fuel. The acute shortages of spare parts and fuel which followed the withdrawal of US aid therefore caused disruption to established marketing patterns and may have been an important reason for declining production and marketed surpluses, as well as reports of produce perishing for lack of transport to processing facilities, after the war. On the other hand, the development of good roads is an important factor in helping to create a national market and the American roads have certainly been a lasting legacy to the economy of Southern Vietnam in this respect.

Roads have so far remained a less important means of transport than water in one key economic region – the Mekong delta. They are expensive to maintain in the delta zone because of flood damage and, to date, no bridges have been built across the two main distributaries of the Mekong river, so traffic bottlenecks occur at the main ferry crossings.[89] Water transport has therefore remained the most important mode of transport here. Yet the network of canals and irrigation channels fell into disrepair during the war:[90] the decline in the export of rice meant that neither private capital nor the State retained an interest in maintenance or repair of war damage. This in turn contributed to the difficulties experienced in obtaining surplus grain to feed the urban populations of the South.

The experience of North Vietnam in the early 1960s, and earlier in China shows that increases in output were made possible by improved organisation of labour for irrigation works within the collectives. Conditions vary in the Mekong delta – extensive development of farming is still possible in some areas but future expansion in some low-lying parts requires efforts to prevent sea-water intrusion and, in more densely populated areas, increases in intensive farming will depend upon the possibility of mobilising labour for construction and maintenance of hydraulic works. Large-scale irrigation schemes have been carried out by the State in South Vietnam since 1975 (for example the Dau Tieng scheme in Tay Ninh province). Smaller schemes are considered best carried out cooperatively since this provides a framework for continuous maintenance. Up to 1985, it had not proved possible to establish a widespread and effective system for carrying out these works in the Mekong delta – partly because such necessarily cooperative activities have been linked to the creation of production collectives which, as we shall see in subsequent chapters, have suffered from serious organisational problems. It seems likely that the restoration and expansion of irrigation works was correspondingly delayed. (Under the French regime, as under Thieu, this work was carried out by *corvée* labour and encountered considerable peasant resistance.)

During the war, the railway network fell into almost complete disuse, apart from a few short stretches such as that from Saigon to Bien Hoa, because of its vulnerability to sabotage.[91] The main line from north to south has now been restored, sometimes after decades of neglect and decay, but the network still experiences difficulties[92] due to poor track-bedding, weak bridge structures, inadequate rolling-stock, and is subject to an investment constraint in so far as railways are relatively capital-intensive. The United States has opposed allocation of multilateral aid funds for railway reconstruction since 1979, arguing that such aid would have military implications.

South Vietnam suffered from chronic power-shortages during the period under consideration, usually caused by repeated sabotage of the transmission lines from Da Nhim hydro-electric power station in the central highlands which, in the early 1960s, supplied the majority of Saigon's electric power.[93] To overcome the problem, a series of power stations were built closer to the city and, since North Vietnam contains virtually all of the country's coal reserves, these were mainly diesel- or gas-fired, a further element causing dislocation at a time of actual fuel shortages after the war.[94] Asian Development Bank loans for improving power distribution were suspended in 1975 and not reactivated until 1978.[95] Since the end of the war, the main focus of energy policy in the South has been on improving the country's hydro-electric potential. Some power stations have been converted to coal, which can be supplied by North Vietnam, and exploration for oil and gas in the South China Sea continued. Although there were expectations of significant oil and gas discoveries after 1973, these did not come to fruition until a decade later.

EMPLOYMENT

In writings on the economy of South Vietnam, frequent references occur to the existence of labour shortages as one of the major economic effects of the war.[96] In the case of industry, it is certainly true that the more highly-skilled elements of the workforce tended to be drafted into the armed services so that industry experienced difficulties in obtaining this sort of labour. There were also complaints from Vietnamese employers of inability to compete with higher wages offered by US military and civilian contractors. In the case of unskilled labour, it is likely that women, who tend to be employed extensively in areas like food-processing and textiles in other Asian countries, were more attracted by the higher remuneration offered in the services sector. But the shortages of labour coincided with rather high rates of official unemployment and, in the urban areas, low rates of labour force participation (see page 77) which suggest that the reasons for the shortages were more complicated than supply and demand for labour at a given wage.

One element of a possible explanation is the fact that in 1960, 88 per cent of the workforce were employed in traditional agriculture.[97] Most of the skilled workers by 1974 had, therefore, acquired their skills (as well as the necessary attitudes to discipline and use of time suited to factory or office life rather than farming) through military and related service. Most people entering the urban labour force in South Vietnam in the 1960s were recent arrivals from war-torn rural areas, without any prior industrial background. In the climate of Saigon and other cities there were many opportunities for survival in illegal and semi-legal activities – petty trade, prostitution, drug dealing, black marketeering – which offered, if not higher incomes, greater freedom of life-style than factory labour.[98] Inability of workers to obtain the necessary means of subsistence other than by sale of labour power to an employer is a vital pre-condition for the creation of a disciplined industrial workforce. Absence of this condition is likely to cause problems of high labour turnover, absenteeism, slowing down of work pace (especially where a division of labour based on refinements of traditional artisan techniques allows workers a degree of control over the labour process). These factors might explain the co-existence of labour shortage in industry with a large pool of (officially) unemployed pople in South Vietnam. If so, low productivity of labour might also have been a reason for the failure of manufacturing employers to offer better wages and conditions to attract more labour. This is an area which requires more investigation than has been possible here.

Labour shortages experienced during the war period were clearly shortages relative to demand. After the war, with the release of personnel from the armed forces in particular, there would have been a far more highly skilled workforce available than the current level of industrial development warranted, especially given that the ARVN relied very much on technical sophistication. Far from constituting a shortage then, there would have been a pool of skilled labour well in excess of demand and a significant source of discontent, possibly influencing the exodus of 'boat people' in the latter half of the 1970s.

By 1974, nearly 1.2 million persons were employed by the South Vietnamese Government in various military, para-military and civil service roles. These represented 19 per cent of the total estimated employed labour force.[99] Agriculture, forestry and fishing, in that year took 56 per cent, industry three per cent, services 23 per cent.[100] Officially, over one and a half million, or 20 per cent of the total workforce, were unemployed, the share of unemployment being slightly higher among urban occupations.[101]

While official unemployment stood at 20 per cent, the amount of surplus labour was actually much higher. For example, labour-force participation rates for the urban areas were measured at only 25 per cent of the population, compared with a rural rate of 44 per cent (possibly reflecting higher female participation).[102] A more accurate reflection of surplus labour in the economy could be gained by taking into account that part of the urban population not accounted for in the official labour force statistics. This may involve including some women – though among the urban poor, domestic labour can be a crucial element in family survival when goods and services cannot be purchased in the market. Such unpaid labour would become even more vital in the post-war situation of absolute shortages. A more important group to include are the many thousands engaging in illegal and semi-legal occupations. While some of these have undoubtedly continued in the same activities since the war (attracted by the high returns from smuggling and black marketeering in a shortage economy), there have also been strenuous efforts by the Government to transfer people to more productive occupations.

The extent of the post-war labour surplus can only be fully realised, however, when the service and defence sectors of the economy are also taken into account. In agriculture and industry, actual employment in 1974 represented only about 40 per cent of the RVN's available and potential labour resources. Demobilisation of the armed forces, for example, released over 700 000 members of the regular army.[103] The enormous expansion of commercial and other services under the Diem and Thieu regimes also provided jobs in many areas which would become redundant under a socialist regime, while others would receive low priority in the new situation. The impact of the changeover is uncertain because many administrative and other personnel (for example, in foreign trade, banking) were retained in order to ensure continued circulation of goods. The necessity to make extensive use of the skilled employees of this sector (in spite of their attachment, often, to ideologies incompatible with those of the new regime) was increased by the success of the CIA-directed Phoenix Program in eliminating much of the NLF's government infrastructure between 1968 and 1975. Moreover, many of the northern cadres who came south in 1975 to fill the gap were inexperienced in and inadequately prepared for the different conditions prevailing there.

In the rural areas too there was considerable unemployment, though slightly less, as a percentage of the rural labour force, than in the cities.[104] Here too, there were labour shortages brought about by the combined effects of drafting men into the armies of both sides, rural–urban migration during the war and a relatively high land-labour ratio in the Mekong delta. Rather than adversely affecting production, however, these changes may have encouraged more mechanised farming.[105] It seems likely, in view of the rather high rate of official rural unemployment, that this effect was unevenly spread.

The overall performance of the South Vietnamese economic system demonstrates that there existed a potentially strong economy which had been fettered in its development by the prevailing set of social relations, by the degeneration into civil war and by American intervention, but which retained a certain vitality underneath this, given that agriculture and transport could be rehabilitated and foreign exchange could be more effectively conserved. One of the key features of the development of the productive forces in South Vietnam during the 1960s and 1970s was the degree of penetration of society by commodity relations, based not on a deepening division of labour between agriculture and industry, but on the rapid expansion of aid-financed imports, largely to meet the needs of an inflated urban services sector, but in the later years reaching the rural areas as well. It is to this question of aid dependency that I now turn.

DEPENDENCE OF THE REGIME ON THE UNITED STATES

In order to comprehend fully the magnitude of the economic problems facing South Vietnam after 1975, it is necessary to dwell on the extent of the Southern regime's dependence on American (and other Western) economic assistance. Some indications of this have already been given, but they barely scratch the surface.

As mentioned above, South Vietnam's export income contributed virtually nothing to its balance of payments position (Figure 3.5). The two major exports of earlier years, rice and rubber, both suffered badly from war damage and lack of investment, especially after 1963–4. Whereas at its peak in 1960 export income had covered as much as 38 per cent of import expenditures, by 1970 the figure was reduced to less than two per cent (though improving slightly subsequently).[106] On top of these unimpressive export figures there was, between 1956 and 1972, a net outflow of private long-term capital.[107]

On the other side of the account, little effort was made at any stage to restrict the growth of imports, particularly of consumer goods. Apart from the well-known propensity of the Saigon élite to buy French wine, luxury limousines and other ingredients of the *dolce vita*, some more basic imports were also necessary from a political and economic point of view. Owing to the lack of productive investment and the impossibility of supplying the rapidly expanding urban population with the necessities of life from domestic sources, high levels of imported consumer goods provided the means to fill this gap (the few industries

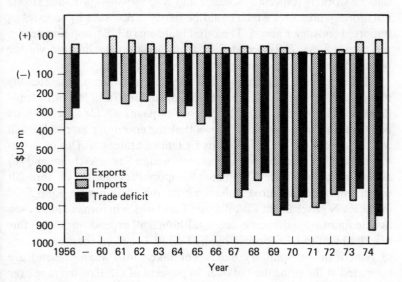

Figure 3.5   South Vietnam: balance of trade
Source: Tinh Hinh Kinh Te Mien Nam 1955–75, Ho Chi Minh City, 1979, p. 33.

established, however, did tend to be import-substituting). Both Diem and many of his American advisers regarded imported consumer goods as an essential ingredient of their anti-Communist programme – if people were attracted to communism by their poverty, supplying them with full shops and rising standards of consumption might eliminate the problem. Most advisers saw these imports as a stop-gap measure; in the long run an increase in productive investment would be required. Short-term contingencies of the war meant, however, that longer-term plans tended to receive low priority in the field.[108] Continuing pressure from American economic advisers to shift imports more towards investment goods and to reduce luxury consumer imports was vigorously resisted by the economic élite.[109] While the Americans hoped for doses of 'rationality' in economic policy, these proved impossible to achieve in view of the nature of the political regime in which United States political leaders continued to have confidence.

There were other, economic, factors as well as the political considerations contributing to the maintenance of persistently high levels of consumer good imports. These related to the need to suppress inflationary tendencies in the economy. Large budget deficits, brought about by accelerated repression of the NLF rather than by any goal of rapid economic expansion, and the rising monetary incomes of unproductive workers (especially soldiers and civil servants) provided strong inflationary pressures which could be partly suppressed by supplies of imported consumer goods. The rapid build-up of US troop numbers in the period 1965–7 also created a strong inflationary impulse via the piastre expenditures of the highly paid US personnel.

In consequence, the import bill for South Vietnam rose steadily throughout the period, reaching $US925.5 million in 1974 (with a trade deficit of $US853 million). The balance of payments for selected years is set out in Table 3.3 which shows that the enormous external deficit was financed directly and indirectly by United States aid. This took two forms: (a) US Government expenditures within South Vietnam and (b) direct grants under the Commercial Import Program (CIP), through which importers acquired dollars by paying their piastre equivalent into a RVN government Counterpart Fund which in turn could be used to help finance the domestic deficit (although all expenditures from this fund had first to be approved by the US).[110] Together, these two forms of American aid (military aid is not taken into account here) are estimated at the equivalent of over 30 per cent of GNP on average over the period 1964–9.[111]

While total aid (including military aid) levels fell after 1972 with the

Table 3.3 South Vietnam's balance of payments and US aid: selected years ($USm)

	1964	1968	1969	1970*
(1) Imports c.i.f.	−323	−669	−818	−780
(2) Exports	49	42†	32†	20
(3) Trade balance	−274	−627	−785	−760
(4) Balance on services (excl. US Government expenditures)	−2	−112	−69	−141
(5) Balance on private capital and transfers, Government capital n.i.e., errors and omissions	11	−145	−125	5
(6) Economic aid and loans except US economic grants	15	22	20	25
(7) Monetary authorities (+ = decline in assets)	39	0	60	30
(8) Total of (3) to (7)	−233	−862	−899	−841
(9) US Government expenditure on goods and services	22	386	411	408
(10) US economic aid grants	211	476	488	433
(11) Total US expenditure and grants	233	862	899	841

*Estimate; †Includes $26m in 1968 and $17m in 1969 of petroleum products resales to the US.
Source Asian Development Bank, *Southeast Asia's Economy in the 1970s* London: Longman, 1971, pp. 596–7.

United States' retreat from active combat, both CIP and PL 480 aid continued to increase in value, right up to the last minute.[112] This meant that the urban middle classes were able (at least in part) to maintain an artificially high standard of living even in the face of economic depression and successive military collapses of the regime.

In addition to maintenance of high consumption-levels through imports, there was also the heavy reliance by industry and agriculture on imported equipment and inputs. Mention has already been made of this factor in relation to industry, but some comment is also needed on the situation in agriculture. In the early 1970s, perhaps in belated recognition of the importance of agriculture and the failure of the Strategic Hamlet programme to 'pacify' the rural population, the Thieu regime began to promote the application of 'green revolution' techniques to small-scale farming. While it is difficult to disentangle the effects of this from those of the land reform also carried out by Thieu, reduced levels of military activity in the 1970s, or the weather, there do appear to have been improvements in output at this time. More important from the present point of view is the fact that the introduction of a capitalist-type 'green revolution' involved a substantial increase in imported capital equipment and other modern inputs.[113] Chemical fertilisers, for example, were hardly produced at all in South Vietnam. While some small-scale plants may have existed,[114] the construction of a major production facility at An Hoa had to be stopped in 1964 because of lack of security, and output evidently was too small to warrant the publication of separate statistics prior to 1975.

An additional difficulty for the post-war economy of South Vietnam arises from the fact that the country relied for its imported goods on a handful of principal sources. In the last years of the regime, approximately 40 per cent of the imports came from the United States.[115] Japan accounted for a further 25 per cent while France and Taiwan together accounted for another 15–20 per cent.[116] This was largely a result of deliberate United States policy to tie imports under the CIP to exports from the US and its close allies in the region (known as Code 941 countries), and to the transport of goods in the ships of those countries.[117] In March/April 1971 the US decreed that goods in many categories could only be imported from the United States.[118] Thus, figures published in mid-1971 showed that 84.9 per cent of US aid-funded imports came from the USA itself, 12 per cent from Taiwan and 1.8 per cent from South Korea.[119] Concentration of import-sourcing in this way made the implementation of a US-sponsored economic blockade against Vietnam in the post-1975 era somewhat easier, especially where aid-tied goods were not readily substitutable (e.g. certain capital goods and spare parts).

As far as foreign investment is concerned, the available data are rather sketchy. At the end of French rule, as mentioned earlier, most non-agricultural enterprises, rubber plantations and a substantial portion of rice land were either French-owned or, in the case of commerce, Chinese-owned. After 1956, ethnic Vietnamese also began to own enterprises, chiefly in the highly profitable import business, and a number of state-run and joint state-private industrial firms were established.[120] Foreign ownership was thus diluted, but remained very high.[121] The concentration of ownership in French hands had also been somewhat loosened, the main new investors being Japanese, American and South Korean.[122] But in spite of frequent statements by the Government aimed at encouraging foreign investment (even more after the death of Diem, who was always suspicious of foreign control over the economy), there was barely a trickle.[123]

Some idea is obtainable from Table 3.4 of the types of enterprise in which foreign capital was chiefly invested. Given the high levels of concentration of output in the Vietnamese industrial sector and the large size of foreign capital invested compared with the size of the main firms operating in this sector,[124] the nationalisation of foreign and comprador assets which took place in 1975–6 could have had quite a disruptive effect on the flow of funds and technology to this area of the economy – depending on the nature of the foreign investment and the relationship between parent company and Vietnamese subsidiary. In fact, in the manufacturing sector, the two French-owned firms in beverages and two more in tobacco controlled 99 per cent and 100 per cent of (legal) output respectively.[125] Vietnamese ownership was more prominent, however, in foodstuffs, where of the seven companies controlling 97 per cent of output, only one was foreign controlled (American), and in textiles.

Foreign investment was also prominent in the fisheries sector. In construction, several large American firms had, on their departure in 1972, bequeathed to the South Vietnamese Government's VECCO (Vietnam Engineering and Construction Company) a large part of their plant and equipment, making VECCO the largest facility of its kind in South-East Asia. It was also, however, highly dependent upon imported inputs.

Table 3.4   Distribution of foreign capital by sector, 1974

Sector	$VNm	% of capital
Industry	20 376.3	49
Foodstuffs, tobacco and beverages	5 519.9	13
Fisheries	3 289.1	8
Forestry	970.5	2
Livestock and agriculture	433.9	1
Services	8 678.7	21
Banking	2 090.8	5
Commerce	198.2 ⎱	0.6
Insurance	49.3 ⎰	
Total	41 615.4	99.6*

*Does not add to 100% due to rounding.
Source   *Tinh Hinh Kinh Te Mien Nam 1955–75* (THKTMN) (Ho Chi Minh City: Institute of Social Sciences, 1979), p. 54.

Perhaps the best overall picture of the development of South Vietnam's dependence on external assistance is obtained by looking at the relationship between national expenditure and income (Figure 3.6).

Public and private consumption expenditure, taken together, consistently exceeded Gross Domestic Product – averaging 103.5 per cent of GDP over the period 1960–72. Gross capital formation, that is, the expenditure item from which any increase in the productive capacity of the economy must come, remained tiny compared to both GNP (10.6 per cent) and total expenditure (9.3 per cent). It must be remembered too, that this category includes expenditure on replacement of worn-out plant and equipment, including war damage, so that any net addition to the capital stock can only be obtained after allowing for this. Total expenditure averaged 114.1 per cent of GDP during this period. The difference between national income (GDP) and domestic expenditure levels $(C + I + G)$ is accounted for by the external deficit $(X - M)$, financed by US aid.

The consequences of the persistent gap between expenditure and

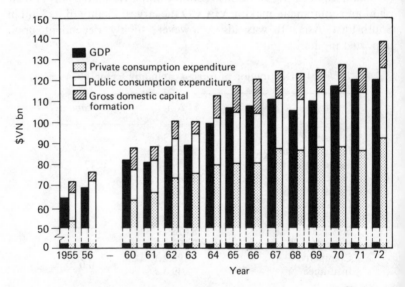

Figure 3.6   South Vietnam: GDP and total domestic expenditure (constant 1960 prices)
Source: Tinh Hinh Kinh Te Mien Nam 1955–75 (Ho Chi Minh City: 1979) p. 114; and Chi Do Pham, *Inflationary Finance in War-time South Vietnam 1960–72,* University of Pennsylvania, PhD thesis 1976, p. 29.

income were serious in view of the subsequent withdrawal of the American aid.

The problem lay in the high rate of GDP growth needed to eliminate this gap without inducing cuts in spending. Otherwise, the reduction of aid levels would entail squeezing of one or more of the expenditure categories. Private consumption was the most obvious target for paring (if a high rate of growth was to be achieved) since the rate of investment was already low – although it might have been possible to achieve expansion at the same or even lower rate of investment by more effective use of given increments to capital stock. Such improvements can be brought about by lowering the capital–output ratio by, for example, better organisation of labour, improved incentives to labour, better management, recycling of waste and a shift in the allocation of resources towards sectors of the economy with lower capital–output ratios (as in agriculture, and artisan industry).[126] Such improvements in the utilisation of capital would, in any case, be vital because cuts in consumption levels can have a very adverse consequence for the growth rate via their effect on incentives and labour productivity. Luxury consumption is a category which can be pruned with more safety, although the borderline between what has become socially necessary (for example, through changes in culturally-determined consumption patterns) in an economy like that of South Vietnam, and what is 'luxury', would have to be treated with care. Public consumption would also be difficult to decrease because expenditure on health, education and welfare could be expected to take up much of the funds previously allocated to internal security matters by the Thieu regime. Security, however, was also liable to remain a high priority under the new Government and this has certainly proven to be the case.

Reduced per capita consumption can be avoided, even though the share of consumption in national income is compressed, if labour productivity is rising faster than the rate of growth of employment and the increase in the share of investment is gradual, allowing real wages and peasant incomes to remain constant or even rise a little during the transition. However, it is doubtful whether such conditions prevailed in Southern Vietnam in the post-war years, in view of the countrywide stagnation in agricultural output and the slowdown in the growth rate of industry during the years of the Second Five Year Plan (1976–80) at the same time as efforts were being made to increase employment rapidly. Without productivity growth the investment rate cannot be raised without simultaneously reducing per capita consumption.[127] However, there is a consumption constraint implicit in socially-defined minimum subsistence levels which, whether or not they are close to a physical subsistence minimum, will cause an adverse effect on labour productivity if they are reduced. If the investment rate is raised to a greater extent than is implied by the consumption constraint, then the effect can be to raise the capital–output ratio with little or negative effect on the rate of growth.

The new regime in Southern Vietnam was therefore faced with an extremely difficult problem. On the assumption that no reduction was possible in the rate of government consumption expenditure and that no new external aid was available, an attempt simply to maintain the investment rate at about 10 per cent would raise the prospect of reducing the share of private consumption in national expenditure by up to 15 percentage points. Raising the investment rate beyond 10 per cent of GDP would lead to further reductions in the share of consumption. Not only would this threaten the growth process itself, but it could (and did) give rise to political problems, as those who initially were willing to accept the new regime became disillusioned in the face of falling growth rates and declining living standards.[128]

The Vietnamese government did, in the mid- to late-1970s, emphasise the importance of developing agriculture, particularly export crops, as the best way to promote rapid growth in the post-war situation. This was consistent both with the 'economic complementarity' thesis outlined in the Introduction to this book and with Vietnamese leaders' understanding of the importance of the division of labour between industry and agriculture in the economic growth process. The Government was also well aware of the consumption constraint on raising the rate of investment, and planned to use labour accumulation schemes, reorganisation of labour and means of production within a collective framework as a means of raising labour productivity and maintaining a fairly low capital–output ratio, as had been done in the North earlier. But at the same time the Second Five Year Plan, introduced in 1976, effectively continued the emphasis on investment in heavy industry in the North,[129] placing strains on consumption which affected the overall growth rate of the economy and, as I shall argue later in this book, the institutional framework within which policies were implemented in the South also had a counter-productive effect.

A further point needs to be made that the expenditure gap shown in Figure 3.6 does not reflect the extent to which the production of GDP itself was dependent upon the huge import programme in the RVN. The US-led economic blockade after the war inevitably meant considerable disruption to the production process – acute shortages of inputs for industry and agriculture, inability to obtain spare parts, withdrawal of experienced and technical personnel (including Vietnamese refugees). Some sectors would require substantial amounts of investment in the production of local raw materials and spare parts, or a big increase in exports (also often requiring investment or – as with rubber – a long gestation period) in order to overcome the foreign exchange shortage before production could be restored to pre-1975 levels. Other sectors could recover more quickly. Considerable use was made of recycled military hardware and other stocks left over from the old regime, though the supply of these was necessarily of limited duration. Subject to the above qualifications about improved effectiveness of investment, and depending upon the degree of capital intensity involved, the rapid recovery of industry would therefore require an even greater contraction in the share of consumption than suggested above. In any case, domestic production of certain consumer goods was likely to fall in the early period after the end of the war. In an economy already affected by recession following reductions in US expenditure, further falls in output would have a reverse multiplier effect. Dramatic rises in prices of fertiliser and fuel after the 1973 oil 'shock' were also bound to affect food production during 1975, adding to the consumer goods shortages.

All these consequences could be alleviated to some extent if American aid had been replaced by aid from alternative sources such as the Soviet Union or North Vietnam, or by adoption of an appropriate economic strategy which reduced the necessity of squeezing consumption. Taking into account the size of surplus labour power and the small (possibly even negative) economic surplus produced, one can see that good organisation and efficient planning after 1975 could, in principle, have transformed the situation from one of a large *potential*, but low *actual* economic surplus into its opposite, in a medium-term perspective. However, the Five Year Plan adopted by the newly-formed Socialist Republic of Vietnam in 1976, followed the practice, established in the former Democratic Republic, of emphasising rapid growth of heavy industry, albeit to a lesser extent than in some previous plans. This plan was designed in the apparent expectation of receiving foreign aid (and some investment) from the Soviet Union and China, as well as the United States. Since little aid did in fact become available from Western sources, and Chinese aid was soon terminated, the bottlenecks of the southern economy had to be met, as much as possible out of loans from CMEA countries and from domestic resources. Efforts were also made to achieve growth in the South through labour absorption and reduction in the capital–output ratio. But the two strands of policy were inconsistent: local reductions in capital–output ratios were offset (or more than offset) by the overall policy of 'heavy industry first'.

These policies are the subject matter of later chapters. It is hard to avoid the conclusion in the interim, however, that in view of the artificially high standards of consumption and continuing political instability of the South after 1975 and the failure, for whatever reason, to achieve a substantial increase in the agricultural marketed surplus of the Mekong delta, the main burden of providing the extra domestic resources under conditions of a 'heavy industry first' strategy, must have fallen on the (already low) living standards in North Vietnam.

Appendix 3.1   Investment and output at constant 1960 prices

Year	GDP $VNbn*	Gross investment $VNbn	Investment rate (Share in GDP) %	Depreciation rate† %	Net investment rate %
1955	64.2	4.9	7.6		
1956	69.4 (8.1)	4.0	5.8		
1960	81.8	10.3	12.6		
1961	81.1 (−0.8)	7.2	8.9	52.5	4.2
1962	88.7 (9.4)	9.7	10.1	50.0	5.1
1963	89.5 (0.9)	6.7	7.5	62.0	2.8
1964	99.8 (11.5)	11.1	11.1	36.8	7.0
1965	108.0 (8.2)	12.7	11.8	29.2	8.5
1966	108.5 (0.5)	15.7	14.5	24.8	11.8
1967	110.7 (2.0)	14.0	12.7	22.4	9.7
1968	105.8 (−4.6)	12.4	11.7	41.7	5.1
1969	110.2 (4.2)	10.9	9.9	40.0	6.2
1970	117.5 (6.6)	12.6	10.7	38.9	6.8
1971	120.7 (2.7)	11.2	9.3		
1972	120.3 (−0.3)	13.1	10.9		

*Figures in brackets are annual growth rates (%);
†Provision for consumption of fixed capital as a share of Gross Domestic Capital Formation.
Source   GDP from *THKTMN*, p. 114; Gross investment and Investment rate calculated from Chi Do Pham, *Inflationary Finance in Wartime South Vietnam 1960–72*, University of Pennsylvania, PhD thesis, 1976, p. 29 (compiled from National Bank sources); Depreciation rate from National Institute of Statistics, *Nien Giam Thong Ke Viet Nam* (Statistical Yearbook), Saigon, 1969, 1972 (in Vietnamese and English).

4 Southern Agriculture

In this chapter, the strengths and weaknesses of the Southern agricultural economy are surveyed in more detail than was possible in the last. We have already seen that the productive capacity of the South was heavily concentrated in the rural sector by the end of the war and that this sector played an important role in Vietnamese thinking on unification on account of the large economic surplus it had produced during the colonial period. To begin with, I review briefly the way in which the leadership in Hanoi saw the economic potential of this sector at the time of political unification of the country. Next, the changes which took place prior to 1975 are reviewed and the implications of these for the process of transformation and construction are examined. The final section looks at the period since 1975, focusing on the way in which major problems were tackled by policy makers and in which the peculiar features of the South have influenced Vietnamese thinking on the whole question of the socialist transformation of agriculture. This section also draws on interviews conducted at various agricultural enterprises and government departments during late 1985.

AGRICULTURE IN VIETNAM'S DEVELOPMENT STRATEGY AFTER 1975

The alternatives which faced the country's economic planners after Liberation in 1975 were limited on account of the legacy of 30 years' war and successive French and American occupations. In the first place, there was no heavy industrial base. That created in North Vietnam had been seriously damaged by American bombardments and would itself require extensive renovation before it could make much impact on the supply of capital goods for industrial development in the South. Imports would also be restricted in view of the reductions in aid levels (both Western and Chinese) and imposition of the American embargo. In the second place, the existence of artificially high consumption standards in South Vietnam and the possibility of rising political instability if these were reduced too far, meant that it would not be advisable to base a development strategy upon the traditional 'heavy industry priority' model which had been favoured by the

Democratic Republic of Vietnam.[1] In view of the previous Southern dependence on imported consumer goods, efforts would now have to focus on the development of agriculture and light industry in order to satisfy the basic consumer needs of the population. The large urban populations, in particular, had depended heavily on imported food during the war period (this applied to the North as well as the South) and it became imperative for the Government, given the tremendous agricultural potential of the country, to achieve self-sufficiency in food in order to conserve valuable foreign exchange. Moreover, the agricultural sector could eventually supply raw materials to the industrial sector and, directly or indirectly, provide the basis for greatly increased export income. Because of their relatively low capital–output ratios, agriculture and light industry could generate increased income rather more quickly than heavy industry.

A further important reason for a shift in the development strategy was the change, after 1975, in the nature and extent of external resources available to the country. During the war North Vietnam, like the South, had been heavily supported by foreign aid injections, primarily from China and the Soviet Union. Following the end of the war in the South, aid from China began to be wound down (it ceased altogether in 1978). Economic assistance from the Soviet Union, by now the largest contributor, mainly took the form of loans rather than grants. The grants and subsidies previously accorded to South Vietnam were, of course, almost completely eliminated. Vietnam was thus now faced with having to find more domestic sources of accumulation where in the past it had relied to a large extent on external ones. In view of the extensive wartime destruction of industry in the North and the dependence of the tiny Southern industrial sector upon external resources, the chief possibilities for quickly acquiring domestic surpluses for accumulation lay in agriculture, particularly in the traditional surplus-producing area of the Mekong delta.

The 1976–80 national Five Year Plan therefore represented a shift in emphasis in economic strategy away from the priority previously given in the DRV to the development of an independent capital goods sector and towards a policy under which agricultural development was stressed *as a means* of achieving eventual industrialisation. This shift is reflected in statements such as the one by Pham Hung (member of the Political Bureau) at the 4th Party Congress in December 1976[2] that the

> primary task of the second 5-year plan is to highly concentrate the forces of the entire country and all branches and echelons on

developing all latent potentials concerning labour, land and material bases to bring about a giant leap forward in agricultural development, considering production of grain and food the main concern . . .

In a similar vein, an article in the Party journal *Tap Chi Cong San*, in September 1977, argued that in the past the leadership had failed to see the essential connection between industry and agriculture and had concentrated one-sidedly on developing industry;[3] instead industrial development should be made to serve the collectivisation movement in agriculture.

One should not overestimate the importance of this shift in emphasis, however. There appears to have been some initial misplaced optimism concerning the possibility of obtaining reconstruction aid from the United States which encouraged the preparation of ambitious investment plans. The growing conflict with China and military involvement along the Cambodian border from 1975 onwards also meant that Vietnamese leaders were anxious to push ahead with modernisation of the economy as rapidly as possible and these factors may help to explain the timidity of the initial move away from the more traditional policy. As we shall see in Chapter 6, the link between high investment rates and slow growth rates had not yet become apparent to many in the DRV leadership. The share of investment in the national income remained high throughout the period 1976–80 at about 18–19 per cent, figures which are close to or even higher than those of the earlier three and five year plans, and investment in heavy industry in fact rose as a share of national income between 1975 and 1979.[4]

Agricultural output stagnated in the 1970s, however, and the Third Five year Plan (1981–85) ratified at the 5th Party Congress of March 1982, restated and strengthened the focus on smaller and more practical projects in industry, putting the main emphases on agriculture, consumer goods industries (especially textiles and paper), oil and energy, exports and communications.[5] The Fourth Five Year Plan ratified in 1986 for the first time abandoned the 'rational priority to heavy industry' altogether, putting agricultural development first. Thus the change in direction of the development strategy, which began in a small and insufficient way in 1975–6, has been carried much further, often, as we shall see, in the face of stiff resistance from within Party and bureaucracy. In part these changes were a response to a developing crisis of agriculture and industry in the North.[6] It will be argued below, however, that this change of direction was also based upon increasing recognition of the specific conditions existing in South Vietnamese agriculture and the effects these were having on the economy as a whole.

REVOLUTION IN THE RURAL AREAS 1955–75

In the quest for food self-sufficiency, attention inevitably turned to the agricultural potential of South Vietnam, especially the Mekong River delta. A number of factors lay behind this, not least of which were the somewhat higher land–labour ratio in the delta area (compared with the densely populated deltas of northern and central Vietnam), especially in the more recently settled western part,[7] and the possibilities provided by areas of abandoned and previously uncultivated land.[8] Most of these uncultivated lands required considerable preparation before they could be brought into production – land simply abandoned had often reverted to jungle, while some lands held more serious obstacles to development: unexploded bombs and ammunition,[9] chemical residues, erosion.[10] Aside from the new areas which could be opened up for cultivation in the South, it appeared to Party strategists that output of a number of key agricultural products, which had suffered through war damage and lack of investment in the rural sector, could be rapidly increased, especially where imported inputs could be replaced by organic fertilisers and through mobilisation of labour for hydraulic works.

Data on changes in output of selected agricultural products in the period 1955–74 were set out in the previous chapter. It will be recalled that the picture presented differed according to crop, but for most there was expanding output during the early 1960s, followed by stagnation and/or decline through the late sixties – the period of escalation of the war – and then recovery, sometimes dramatic, following the American troop withdrawal and signing of the Paris Peace Accords in early 1973. Table 4.1 gives a little more detail on output and productivity of rice and rubber, the two crops which had formed the backbone of the southern export economy during the colonial period. In the case of rubber the decline in output was marked and continuous on account of the long period before young trees begin producing. In the case of rice, on the other hand, the recovery of output began slightly earlier than for other crops and the factors accounting for this constitute an important background to the post-war developments.

Among these, the issue of conditions of land tenure in South Vietnam was crucial to the success or otherwise of the policies adopted

Table 4.1   Paddy and rubber: area, output and yields 1956–74

| Year | Paddy | | | Rubber | | |
	m ha	*m t*	*t/ha*	*000 ha*	*000 t*	*t/ha*
1956	2.1	2.7	1.33	75	70	0.93
1957	2.7	3.2	1.17	75	62	0.83
1958	2.9	4.0	1.37	76	72	0.95
1959	2.5	3.3	1.32	101	75	0.74
1960	2.3	4.9	2.14	109	77	0.70
1961	2.4	4.6	2.10	126	78	0.61
1962	2.5	5.2	2.10	136	78	0.57
1963	2.5	5.3	2.10	143	76	0.53
1964	2.6	5.2	2.03	135	74	0.55
1965	2.4	4.8	1.99	130	65	0.50
1966	2.3	4.3	1.89	126	49	0.39
1967	2.3	4.7	2.04	116	42	0.36
1968	2.4	4.4	1.82	106	34	0.32
1969	2.4	5.1	2.10	105	28	0.27
1970	2.5	5.7	2.27	106	33	0.31
1971	2.6	6.3	2.41	103	37	0.34
1972	2.7	6.3	2.35	83	20	0.24
1973	2.8	7.0	2.48	68	19	0.28
1974	2.9	7.1	2.48	68	21	0.31

Source   Tinh Hinh Kinh Te Mien Nam 1955–1975, Ho Chi Minh City: Institute of Social Sciences, 1979, pp. 136, 138.

by the new socialist regime after 1975, so it is worth taking some space to describe the changing situation under the Diem/Thieu regimes – especially as it bears on the question of surplus production and appropriation. A second issue of vital importance is the nature of the relationship between the two zones – government-controlled and NLF-controlled – during the war. These two factors played a major role in determining the social and economic structure of Southern Vietnamese agriculture and the development options open to the new Government.

Southern Vietnam had, like the North, a long history of revolutionary activity prior to the French departure in 1955. Under direct French colonial rule from the 1860s (unlike the centre and north which were protectorates), the peasants of Nam Bo (or French Cochin-China) experienced probably the most inequitable distribution of land in the whole country. In the Mekong delta, particularly its western part, French construction of irrigation and drainage works accelerated the opening up of land for cultivation and, although in principle land could belong to those who first cultivated it, in practice a few wealthy French and Vietnamese were able to manipulate the legal and bureaucratic system to gain control of large estates.[11] A system of surplus appropriation through rent grew up and led to the Mekong delta becoming a large rice-exporting region. The export of rice imposed a heavy burden upon the peasantry: there is evidence to suggest that the per capita availability of rice for peasant consumption began to fall at about the time of the First World War[12] while exports continued to rise.

The system of land tenure under the French played no small part in this relative immiseration of the peasantry (by the Great Depression this had become absolute immiseration as per capita consumption fell below the subsistence minimum) since neither tenant nor landlord held any interest in raising productivity of the land through investment. Insecurity of tenure and lack of access to investable surpluses were the reasons in the case of the peasant cultivators, while the non-cultivating landowners were concerned with distribution of the product rather than its production. Many landlords lived in the towns, relying on agents to collect the rent and selling the produce to the Chinese merchants who dominated the grain trade. More importantly perhaps, output could be increased by expanding the area under cultivation, reducing the need to raise productivity of existing land.

Towards the end of the First Indo-China War, however, the Viet Minh (led by the Communist Party) controlled a substantial proportion of the countryside and carried out rent reductions followed by land reform, forcing the larger owners to flee to urban centres. Following American intervention to install Ngo Dinh Diem in power and to prevent the reunification of the country scheduled for 1956 under the Geneva Accords, the South Vietnamese Government undertook its own land reform. Diem's programme, in effect, attempted to reverse the Viet Minh reform since it imposed a very high limit of 115 hectares on individual landholdings and there were many loopholes allowing landowners to maintain even larger holdings.[13]

The Viet Minh presence in the countryside, however, prevented any return to the pre-1946 situation and, after the formation of the National Liberation Front in 1960, more and more areas of the country fell out of Government control. In the many regions in which the NLF had influence, land was either distributed to the cultivators or, in view of the Front's efforts to gain acquiescence of the smaller, 'patriotic' landlords, rents were simply reduced well below the Government's legal maximum of 25 per cent. Sansom found, on the other hand, that in the areas which were most securely controlled by the Government, not only did large landowners retain control of their land, but rents were often well in excess of the legal maximum.[14] Because of NLF success in driving landowners away, rent collection was often carried out during raids on contested areas by Government troops acting as agents of the landlord. The commissions paid for this service formed an important source of additional income for local commanding officers.

All estimates agree that by 1964 a very high percentage of the rural areas of South Vietnam were under the control of the National Liberation Front, or at least 'Contested'. Even as early as 1961, a US Defense Department memorandum stated that 58 per cent of the country was 'under some form of communist control' ranging from harassment and night raids to almost complete administrative jurisdiction.[15] In 1964 the estimates of the government side were: (a) by the US Defense Department, 40 per cent of the territory under 'communist control or predominant influence' and over half the land area in 22 out of 43 provinces (more than three-quarters in eight provinces);[16] (b) according to Nguyen van Thieu, the 'communists' controlled 75 per cent of the countryside;[17] (c) according to the CIA estimate, only 30 per cent of the population were in areas 'now considered pacified'.[18] Wilfred Burchett presumably gave the Front's own assessment of the situation when he claimed that 4 million out of 6.25 million acres of cultivable land and three-quarters of the total land area had been liberated and that half the peasant population of the South were 'masters of the countryside'.[19]

Escalation of the war in subsequent years seems not to have fundamentally altered the situation, at least until after the Tet Offensive of 1968. After 1968 the war entered a new phase while the NLF attempted to rebuild its forces under heavy pressure from the Phoenix Program and other American and South Vietnamese Government schemes. It is significant that the two major offensives during this period, in 1972 and early 1975, were launched by the regular armed forces of the DRV across the 17th parallel, rather than by the Front itself.[20] There are also reports that after 1969, freedom of movement for RVN forces was much greater than before 1968. A CIA estimate of the size of the 'Third Vietnam' at the time of the Paris Peace Agreements, shows NLF control over large areas of the less-populated highlands and Cambodian border regions, but relatively small areas in the more densely populated Mekong delta.[21]

In its liberated areas, the Front attempted to establish the rudiments of a socialist economy, depending upon the degree of security from attack of the area concerned. Land reforms were carried out on the basis of the particular conditions of the area, especially the degree of pressure for land (land–labour ratio), hostility of local landowners, soil productivity. Cadres were told to 'meet the local situation with the land policy that will get the most support and the greatest production'.[22] Mutual aid teams were formed to bring about more productive use of labour and the sharing of tools and draught animals to assist more disadvantaged groups. The NLF land reforms had repercussions on the balance of power at the local level in all but the most securely held government areas since, for reasons of personal safety, only small landowners continued to be able to live in the villages and rent collections fell dramatically.[23] In the liberated zones some state-run enterprises were formed, both in agriculture and handicrafts, as well as in trade to secure sufficient supplies of goods to the troops.

Taxation in the liberated areas of Binh Dinh province (in the south-central coastal region) consisted of 30 kg of rice per individual per annum. But efforts were made to take into account ability to pay in fixing tax rates. In addition, 'the people and the Party must put aside two kilos of rice per individual per month [equivalent to 10 per cent of a minimum consumption ration], and each member of the Armed Forces one kilo a month' to be purchased at official prices for feeding the troops. Households were urged to keep stocks of rice and salt to meet sudden needs.[24] The CIA estimated NLF tax rates at between 5 and 25 per cent of crop yields – the higher rates for politically suspect individuals – and pointed out also that rice was subject to taxation at milling, transport and market stages. Taxes were also imposed on trade to and from NLF areas, with particularly heavy taxes falling on importation of luxury goods.[25] Owners of tea, coffee and rubber plantations also made regular contributions.[26] There is some suggestion that the obstacles to trade between the zones were counter-productive. An attempt to place a ban on food sales to the government-controlled areas was also counter-productive because the liberated areas failed to develop an adequate market for the needs of the peasantry and this caused discontent.[27]

The NLF areas were subjected to an economic blockade by the RVN Government (although officials and soldiers could often be bribed to supply arms and other goods) as well as defoliation and other forms of destruction, particularly in areas considered to contain NLF training camps, hospitals, logistic installations, way stations on infiltration routes and crops grown to support those centres.[28]

At first, the Front also attempted to disrupt the functioning of the RVN economy through an economic blockade aimed at fuelling inflation and creating discontent among urban populations. The transportation of rice, cattle and buffaloes into government-controlled areas was strictly forbidden at one time.[29] Transport routes to Saigon were frequently disrupted in order to prevent movement of rice from the Mekong delta and vegetables from Dalat in the central highlands to the capital as well as rubber from the plantations to augment South Vietnam's meagre export earnings. In some cases merchants voluntarily withheld supplies from the Saigon market because of the risks of transportation.[30] Power supplies to Saigon were also disrupted by sabotage of transmission lines. The NLF's control over Ca Mau province (now part of Minh Hai), the chief source of charcoal fuel, also created problems for the government side.

On the other hand, the NLF attempted to ensure that necessary consumer goods, inputs and military supplies were able to reach their areas from the RVN-controlled zones. It therefore encouraged trading relations between the two zones, particularly the sale of agricultural surplus goods and forestry products in exchange for essential goods such as rice, salt, fish, medicine and kerosene. These policies would appear to have been quite successful, especially in later years when some of the obstacles to two-way trade mentioned above were removed. Even in the earlier years, before 1968, the Americans believed that the NLF controlled a number of commercial enterprises in South Vietnam, including those involved in the marketing of rice and charcoal, in importing consumer goods and drugs and in exporting fish, rice and charcoal.[31] The same intelligence report put the size of the NLF's total revenue collection from the two zones at 'half that raised by the Saigon Government'.

It is clear from the above that the existence of a substantial parallel economy from 1960 onwards had considerable effect on the development of the economy as a whole. In the RVN-controlled areas, the effect would seem to have been manifested chiefly through restricted supplies of rice and other essential commodities to the cities. These shortages were, however, usually offset by US aid-financed imports so that urban discontent was averted in the short-run, though at the expense of increasing the regime's economic and political dependence on the United States. Moreover, efforts by the NLF to place the RVN under economic blockade were more detrimental to the economy of areas under its own control than to those of the Government. Economic growth in these areas presupposed increasing access by peasants to manufactured consumer goods and inputs. Since these could hardly be brought down the Ho Chi Minh trail during the war, they inevitably had to come from local handicraft manufacture or from Saigon. The heavy physical destruction wrought on NLF and 'contested' areas; the fact that these areas often formed pockets entirely surrounded by government-controlled areas or cut off from each other by RVN road blocks; the fluidity in the geographical make-up of the zones – all these militated against deepening of the division of labour between agriculture and industry within the zones themselves. After 1969, in response to peasant discontent resulting from the impossibility of creating an adequate market within autarkic NLF zones, the blockade of the RVN was loosened and many obstacles to two-way trade were removed. The South Vietnamese Government never really succeeded in imposing its own blockade so once the NLF restrictions disappeared trade increased rapidly. Even as early as 1969, an NLF survey of the areas which it controlled in Nam Bo showed that commercialisation of agricultural activity was already quite far advanced: in four villages in the Mekong delta rich peasants (though only a half per cent of the population in the total survey) derived 75 per cent of their income from 'industrial-commercial' activities such as machine-hire and crop handling.[32]

Since the political support of the South Vietnamese regime lay in large measure with the class of landlords, the Government and also the American advisers for the most part refused to recognise that land tenure was a factor in Communist successes. But after the Tet Offensive of 1968 inflicted heavy blows on US and Government morale, the Thieu regime began its attempt to defuse the whole issue by distributing 'Land to the Tillers'. This programme, which was eventually carried out between 1970 and 1973, distributed land to tenant cultivators free, up to a maximum of three hectares in the Mekong delta and one hectare in central Vietnam where population pressure was much greater.

Title to the land given in various Viet Minh and NLF land distributions was finally recognised by the Thieu Government. Landlords were compensated mainly from US funds. By this time, though, land ownership had become a relatively unprofitable source of income for most wealthy Vietnamese. As Gareth Porter points out, there had been a major shift in the concentration of wealth towards the commercial classes and corrupt officialdom.[33] Thieu's reform therefore encountered little resistance from the Government's supporters, a reflection of the fundamental change in the balance of power already brought about by the revolution in the countryside.

It must be emphasised, however, that Thieu's reform did not have much effect in central Vietnam where land ownership remained in contention until the end of the war. Factors contributing to this situation included a more egalitarian distribution of land occupancy, the greater preponderance of small landlords whom the NLF was anxious not to antagonise (60 per cent of landlords were themselves full-time farmers) and the greater proportion of communal land together with lack of consensus about how it should be distributed and who should be compensated.[34] The villages of the central Vietnamese coastal plains followed the pattern of northern Vietnam in that much of the land was communally owned and subject to periodic redistribution among registered householders. Though in practice local notables may have appropriated such land disproportionately, the Thieu land reform posed a difficult question for all villagers since the reform involved permanent alienation of communal land as *private property*, with the attendant risks of bankruptcy for poorer members of the community. In Nam Bo, which had been directly governed by the French and in which most French capital had been invested in agriculture, private property in land was the rule and communal lands were tiny. Here the attitude of peasants to the Thieu reform would have been less ambiguous.

In the longer run the changes in the rural balance of power did not necessarily work to the advantage of the revolution – at least as the Vietnamese leaders perceived its course in the mid- to late-1970s. Land reform in North Vietnam took place between 1953 and 1956 and was followed soon after by a movement towards collectivisation, ostensibly to prevent the emergence of capitalist agriculture and to take advantage of productivity benefits of reorganising labour. In the Mekong River delta of South Vietnam, on the other hand, the distribution of land to individual families took place over a much longer period and in some cases was completed as long as 30 years before the ultimate military defeat of the anti-communist forces. The consequences of this, both for the project of socialist transformation after 1975 and for the development of production in agriculture, were profound: one of the most important aspects being that collectivisation itself was brought under scrutiny.

Figure 4.1 gives some indication of the extent to which the distribution of land ownership in the Mekong delta had changed. The picture of increased equality following the combined NLF and Thieu land reforms is reinforced by the fact that all insecurity of tenure had been eliminated after 1975. Only 23 per cent of the population surveyed in 1978 fell into the category of farm labourer (which includes those owning insufficient land to maintain their families by farming alone).[35]

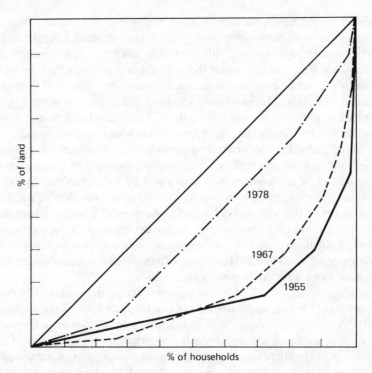

Figure 4.1   Distribution of land ownership in the Mekong delta
Note: Data for 1955 and 1967 are based on titles to land recognised by the
Diem/Thieu Governments and, especially those for 1967, do not reflect actual
tenure conditions.
Source: *Tinh Hinh Kinh Te Mien Nam 1955–75* (Economic Situation of the
Southern Region 1955–75) (Ho Chi Minh City: Institute of Social Sciences,
1979) pp. 124, 126–8; Tran Huu Quang, 'Nhan dien co cau giai cap o nong thon
dong bang song Cuu Long', (Identifying class structure in the rural areas of the
Mekong delta), *Nghien Cuu Kinh Te,* (1982), no. 128, August, p. 32.

Thus the redistribution of land before 1975 would appear, on the basis
of the limited data available, to have produced a much more egalitarian
distribution of land under which the majority of farmers in the delta
had shifted into a 'middle' rather than 'poor' peasant category.

Alongside this shift in land distribution came a change in cultivation
methods – the use of mechanisation and modern inputs increased.
There are several reasons for this: (a) rent reductions meant that for the
first time investible surpluses became available to the peasants themselves;[36] (b) shortages of labour (both family and hired) were brought

about by the disappearance of adult males into the armed forces of both sides or by population outflow to the urban areas;[37] (c) shortages of animal draught power;[38] (d) American aid programmes in agriculture were aimed at increasing the use of modern inputs such as high-yielding varieties, mechanical pumps and rototillers, chemical fertilisers and insecticides. Mechanisation resulting from these combined pressures and inducements was not uniform. According to Sansom,[39] it was concentrated mainly in the upper delta where natural conditions allowed individual farmers more opportunities to make use of high-yielding varieties and multiple cropping techniques. The unevenness of the spread of mechanisation is confirmed by other sources. Le Nhat Quang,[40] for example, says that at the end of the war five of the nine provinces in the Mekong delta had a shortage of draught power and four had more than they needed. At the extremes, An Giang province had 24 000 hp in excess of average requirements, while Cuu Long had a shortage of about 20 000 hp. Even within those provinces which had excess, there were districts with shortages.

Nevertheless, by 1972–3 about a third of the cultivated area had been sown to HYV rice, large numbers of tractors and other farm machines had been imported (those still in operation by 1978 were considered sufficient for basic soil preparation and irrigation requirements of the delta, provided they could be fully utilised and properly maintained[41]) and most farmers had become accustomed to using chemical fertilisers.[42] The widespread use of mechanical pumps was another important feature of agricultural practices in the Mekong delta before 1975. Le Nhat Quang cites Ministry of Agriculture figures to the effect that in 1977 there were about one million hp of privately owned motors for pumps and boats.[43] Virtually all this equipment was imported: between 1968 and 1973, 8568 large and small tractors, 12 359 rototillers, 5575 rice mills, 3549 motorised insecticide sprays and 59 175 hand sprays, 73 474 water pumps and engines, 549 harvesters and threshing machines and 1183 mowers were imported.[44]

The extent of mechanisation is important because it is one of the chief areas of contrast between the Mekong delta in 1975 and North Vietnam in 1959 when collectivisation began there. Whereas in the latter case substantial improvements in yields had been made possible by the collective reorganisation and mobilisation of labour – largely involving the labour-intensive construction and maintenance of irrigation works – in the Mekong delta peasants were already able to achieve yield increases via individually-owned labour-*saving* devices. The immediate economic benefits of collectivisation would not have been so apparent to these peasants as they were to their much poorer, unmechanised colleagues in the North.

It has often been said that the land reforms carried out in places like Taiwan and South Korea and the relatively equal distribution of land in Japan formed the basis for the extraordinarily high productivity of peasant rice cultivation in those countries. It seems that a similar process was in the making in South Vietnam in the early 1970s. In contrast to the experience of the first three countries, however, the changed land tenure situation in Vietnam came about through revolutionary pressure, in the face of protracted resistance from landlords and their political allies. The paradox of this revolutionary development is that, in the Mekong delta at least, it has created the conditions for the development of a strong privately-based agricultural system. Therefore, the problem facing new Vietnamese policy makers in 1975 was not only one of how to continue to develop South Vietnamese agricultural *production* in the face of acute shortages of imported inputs, but also one of how to assess the potential of these social and political changes for achieving socialism.

SOUTHERN AGRICULTURE AFTER 1975

The Communist Party did not, however, immediately look upon the changes in the South as posing any special problems. It saw the key to agricultural development, as in the North after 1956, in the construction of large-scale collective and state farms. The main form of accumulation would come about via utilisation of large existing labour reserves to carry out major construction works of clearing and reclaiming land, irrigation systems, roads and other necessary infra-structure for the new agricultural areas. In the delta itself, the reorganisation of labour through collectivisation would release workers for the important task of rebuilding and repairing the extensive system of irrigation and transport canals. Because of the low-lying terrain of the delta (it is rarely more than two metres above sea level) and the problem of saline intrusion during the dry season, the scale of irrigation works required to make double cropping feasible in the lower delta was rightly thought to require state or collective efforts and could not be left to individual farmers irrigating their own fields. Moreover, the construction of hydraulic works to enable the expansion of mutiple cropping was becoming a more urgent need. Past growth of agriculture in the Mekong delta had been achieved by more extensive farming, through the gradual opening-up of new areas for cultivation. But some parts are now quite densely populated – although not yet approaching the extremely crowded conditions of the northern deltas – and the population density is growing more rapidly than in the north.[45] In a situation of capital scarcity, an important option open to development planners is to increase yields per hectare and per capita production by more intensive cultivation. Since irrigation was the pre-condition for such intensification of agricultural techniques, the organisation of labour by the State for larger works and on a collective basis for smaller schemes was seen in 1975 as the only means whereby the foundation could be laid for the building of 'large scale socialist production' throughout the country.

As a result of earlier Northern successes with irrigation within the institutional framework of cooperative farming and in spite of criticism of these farms then developing in the North, the Party leadership decided in 1976 to go ahead with collectivisation as a means of achieving these changes also in the South. A target date for completion of collectivisation was set for 1980 and in the interim the Government attempted to encourage the process by gaining control over trade in agricultural inputs and outputs from private merchants. Prices for both industrial input sales and grain purchases by the State were based on those prevailing in North Vietnam, rather than on any consideration of the supply and demand situation prevailing in post-war South Vietnam. This proved to be a major cause for the failure of the project, as we shall see below.

The principle that collectivisation should be voluntary was being stressed by officials and so the process was preceded by a phase of preparation involving first, recovery of production from the effects of war and, second, a stage of land 'readjustment' (as opposed to land reform which had already been completed). The land readjustment was aimed less at removing the remaining inequities of land ownership than at 'endowing the peasants with an initial fund' to enable them to participate in the collective economy. Where there was little land to be distributed, the intention was to absorb landless peasants into handicrafts and state enterprises.[46] Nevertheless, as Ngo Vinh Long has pointed out, the recipients of these parcels often lacked the necessary capital equipment and know-how to farm successfully. Land redistribution, without concomitant redistribution of other resources, particularly means of production, meant that Southern peasants – in contrast to the Northern beneficiaries of land reform in the 1950s – often received the land only to re-sell it immediately.[47]

For the longer run, however, the aim of the Government was collectivisation – the whole process of 'achieving socialist transformation' was to be completed by 1980.[48] At this stage, it was assumed in official pronouncements that collective and state-owned agriculture would prove to be inherently superior in providing *economic* benefits as well as political benefits to the peasantry. Recognition was given, however, to the fact that the large number of relatively wealthy peasants in the delta would be unwilling to join collective units if it would put them at a disadvantage economically, hence the need to proceed with caution. But by placing a time limit on the process and by increasing pressure to meet the deadline during 1978, the regime placed local cadres in a sometimes impossible dilemma: how simultaneously to ensure the voluntariness of adherence and still meet the Government's artificially imposed target? As we shall see below, the reconciliation of the two objectives was rarely achieved.

NEW ECONOMIC ZONES

In the meantime, a second option for tapping the South's agricultural potential was open, namely, expansion of the total area under cultivation. The construction of state and collective farms in the New Economic Zones (NEZs) included areas in the vicinity of Ho Chi Minh City which had been heavily bombed and defoliated during the war, as well as more remote, mountainous and war-ravaged terrain along the Cambodian border and in the central highlands. The NEZs were, for the most part, to be highly specialised units producing, for example, rice in the Mekong delta, cotton in the drier areas of Thuan Hai and Phu Khanh provinces, rubber in the foothills of Song Be and Tay Ninh, sugar in Tay Ninh, tea in Lam Dong. It was intended that they should spearhead the development of raw material production for industry and, most importantly, the generation of export income. Since these areas contained no prior set of social relations to be transformed, the Party assumed that collectivisation or state management would be easily put into operation.

By 1980, between 174 and 181 state farms had been established in the South.[49] By 1978, rubber production, which was wholly concentrated in such farms, had regained and surpassed 1967 levels of production[50] (cf. Table 4.1), but for some years after that there was little further increase. This is partly due to the lengthy maturing period of rubber plantations which require six to seven years of growth before latex can be tapped.

The area planted with rubber has, however, increased greatly – to 145 500 hectares in 1984. Much of the area suitable for rubber was badly affected by chemical sprays during the war and this, it is claimed, affects the yield of the mature trees and the growth of young ones on account of soil erosion. This has made living conditions in the new areas difficult (for example, new workers' villages often still lack the usual canopy of fruit trees which can be used to supplement income).

However, not all the problems of new economic zones are attributable to the unique post-war conditions of the South. At first, the state farms experienced a number of problems similar to those already affecting the Northern farms, namely, a tendency to 'go for quantity and breadth rather than intensive cultivation'.[51] Crop and livestock yields tended to be low, reclaimed land was often wasted and reverted to scrub while the standard of living of state farm employees was regarded as 'not good'.[52] Rubber plantations also suffered from severe labour shortages during the late 1970s,[53] paralleling earlier problems of the French planters.

Similar tales were told of the cooperative farms established under the NEZ programme. At first there was a high rate of return to urban areas by former residents who had emigrated to the NEZs. For many, this would have entailed a return to acute economic insecurity which suggests that life, in some of the NEZs at least, must have been hard. In the former free fire zone encircling Ho Chi Minh City, only a few had, by the end of 1979, achieved reasonably good income levels and most were beset with problems, including political ones.[54] Further away, in Dong Nai, where six zones were established (three for people from the southern cities, three for those from northern and central provinces), the planned state subsidy for food and clothing for the first six months had to be extended for three years in some cases because, according to provincial authorities, urban people had no idea how to farm.[55] In Tay Ninh and other provinces near the Cambodian border, many NEZs had to be abandoned during the war with Pol Pot.[56] A partial solution to the problems was found by using the armed forces and 'youth brigades' to clear land and establish basic infrastructure *before* the zones were opened to receive settlers, and this led to more success in holding people. By 1985, according to the Ministry of Agriculture, a total of two million people had moved to New Economic Zones and 600 000–700 000 hectares were in production (out of a million cleared). This was still a far cry from the optimistic targets for population movement and land reclamation of the mid-seventies.[57]

Some progress would seem to have taken place, however. The six zones in Dong Nai province have all achieved self-sufficiency in income and have schools, dispensaries, brick houses. Standards of living were said to have risen to 80 per cent of the average farming level by 1985. Some are in fact well above average on account of their specialisation in high income cash crops like coffee, pepper and soybeans for export. All residents of the zones were in production collectives or cooperatives (compared with 82.3 per cent for the province as a whole), 10 per cent being in the 'higher level' cooperatives (16.5 per cent for the whole province).[58]

The use of new incentive systems in collectives and state farms appears to have been an important factor in improved performance. At Phuoc Hoa rubber plantation in Song Be province, the response to my question about how labour shortages had been overcome was that the introduction of the 'contract system' has increased the 'responsibility' of workers. Under this system workers sign contracts to look after a particular section of the plantation. While the trees are young and the foliage is not too dense, crops like peanuts can be planted between the rows and any income earned from these crops is kept by the workers. This enhances the likelihood that the trees will be adequately fertilised (usually using organic fertiliser purchased from farmers) and the peanuts themselves add nutrients to the soil. In addition, plantations workers are allocated $500 \, m^2$ for their house and garden from which they derive additional income. The introduction of the contract system on the rubber plantations has the advantage that it both reduces the necessity to pay high wages in order to retain workers (under difficult conditions) during a stage when the trees are not yet producing and, by relating income directly to productivity of labour, it overcomes a constant problem of the former plantation owners of lack of incentive. The relatively unskilled and unmechanised nature of plantation work allows workers a large amount of control over the labour process. Productivity can be increased either if the workers are self-motivated or if supervision is very close. As we saw in Chapter 2, the former plantation owners opted for the second path, paying low wages and relying on enforcement of discipline to ensure attendance and productivity maintenance in the face of considerable recalcitrance. By contrast, the contract system applied today has the potential to eliminate a major area of conflict of interest between workers and management over labour productivity.

The contract system is not always used in state farms, however. At a Song Be pig-farm workers are paid by the hour with bonuses if the piglets under each workers' care gain weight beyond a minimum limit.

It would appear that the most important factor accounting for the success of this state farm is that being operated by the provincial, rather than the central, government, it was allowed to find its own market and sources of supply (the farm had exported pigs as far away as North Vietnam). Since my visit in 1985, this provision has been extended to centrally managed state enterprises as well. The province provided investment funds (at the very low interest rate of 0.37 per cent per month), but the company had to buy its own raw materials, usually from farmers in the Mekong delta. It had its own transport team for this purpose. The output of the company (mostly pigs for breeding purposes) was sold directly to the consumer, under both cash and barter arrangements. The herd size had been reduced by a third in the past five years and quality had been improved. This has enabled the company to cope with the problem of electricity shortage, which affected fodder production, and still maintain profitability.

Greater autonomy of decision making and financial responsibility has also benefited the Long An Livestock Company. Here they have been able to circumvent the power shortage by using bio-gas (instead of selling manure to farmers as in Song Be). Supply and marketing arrangements are similar to those used by the Song Be farm and the company is able to retain 50 per cent of its profits (total 256 000 dong in 1984) for its accumulation and bonus funds.

An indication of the variety of institutional arrangements now existing in New Economic Zones can also be seen from an area, still in its earliest stages of development in the Dong Thap Muoi (Plain of Reeds) about 20 km from the provincial capital of Long An. All that has been completed so far is the construction of a road connecting Tan An with a more distant district town and alongside it a canal – as part of a scheme to increase the fresh-water flow and prevent saline intrusion. This area is a swamp. However, there are commercially viable oil-bearing trees (*Melaleuca leucadendron myrtaceae*, known as *tram*). When the road was completed, people began to move into the area to harvest the tram bushes and extract oil using primitive equipment. At present the management of the collective established in the zone aims only to control the marketing of tram oil. Since the state pharmaceutical company has a monopsony position, there is no incentive for workers to sell outside the state marketing structure. But the only state or collective involvement in the production side is via the building of infrastructure, supply of insecticides, tools and R & D. Because the project is in its early stages of development, no tax is collected. Cash incomes were reportedly high, but living conditions in the zone are difficult – there is no electricity, housing is primitive, the distance to the nearest shop is far (no food can be grown, although essentials can be bought from a mobile state shop and travelling pedlars). No mention was made here of the policy applied in other zones, of supplying immigrants with food and house-construction materials and this may be because restructuring of the zone is officially unfinished and because, with tram, there is very little capital requirement and no waiting time before the first harvest.

What all these examples have in common is that the state authorities have greatly reduced their role in enterprise management and concentrated their activities on provision of infrastructure (and sometimes capital) and the setting of product prices. Even in the latter sphere price-setting mechanisms have become much more flexible than in the past, with much greater attention given to the supply and demand component of prices. But the most important development is that by devolving financial responsibility to the enterprise (or individual) level and allowing firms to sign contracts directly with suppliers and customers, the state has provided essential incentives to producers enabling them to improve the quality and profitability of their undertakings. This element of competition has played a key role in reviving production in the NEZs and state farms and, after nearly a decade of costly floundering, they may be able to begin to fulfil the original objective of spearheading export growth.

COLLECTIVISATION

The introduction after 1979 of economic reforms which have allowed more flexibility in the system of individual incentives, and more financial and trading autonomy for agricultural enterprises, appears to have resolved some of the problems earlier plaguing the New Economic Zones. A more serious challenge to the Vietnamese Party's project of transforming agricultural production relations came from the apparent resistance of peasants in the crucial Mekong delta to the idea of joining production collectives and agricultural cooperatives at all. While the collectivisation programme seemingly went ahead quite smoothly in the provinces of central Vietnam after 1976, this was not the case in the Mekong delta.[59] Table 4.2 sets out some data on the progress of collectivisation in the southern and central regions. It shows that formation of collectives was very largely completed in the central coast provinces by the end of 1979. And whereas in the southernmost part of

Table 4.2 Collectivisation of Southern agriculture

Date	Region	% of house-holds	% of cultivated land	Co-ops, no.	Production collectives, no.	Production solidarity teams, no.
July 1979	South	53	38			
	Centre*			1 104	1 564	
	Nam Bo			97†	9 737†	
End 1979	Centre*	83	76	1 114	1 500	
	Nam Bo				12 000	
May 1980	South	50	36			
May 1982	Nam Bo			188	5 637	22 291
End 1983	Nam Bo	<40	33	234	17 720	
Mid 1984	Nam Bo	45.3	38	296	20 341	
End 1984	Nam Bo	57.7	53.4			
March 1985	Nam Bo	72.5	66.1	496	31 206	
End 1985	Nam Bo	90	85	600	38 000	

*Five coastal provinces of Binh Tri Thien, Quang Nam Da Nang, Nghia Binh, Phu Khanh, Thuan Hai.
†Nine provinces of Mekong delta only.
Sources BBC, *Summary of World Broadcasts*, FE/8151/B/8; FE/W1341/A/18; FE/7852/B/8; FE/W1268/A/24; FE/W1292/A18; JPRS 81273, *Vietnam Report* no. 2377, p. 26; JPRS 75723, *Vietnam Report* no. 2189, p. 11; JPRS 74380, *Vietnam Report* no. 2145, p. 12; Chris Nyland, 'The Plan/Market Contradiction . . .', *Journal of Contemporary Asia*, vol. 11 (1981) no. 4, p. 444.

the country, a few cooperatives and 12 000 lower-level production collectives had been established, about half of the latter were not 'working collectively' (that is, existed on paper only). Per capita output expanded during the collectivisation process in the central provinces, but fell by as much as 4.3 per cent a year in the Mekong delta.[60]

Part of the reason for the difference between the two areas of the South may be that, climatic conditions being much more uncertain in the central provinces, peasants stood to gain more by being cushioned by the collective against the consequences of crop losses which could be economically disastrous for individual farmers. A *Nhan Dan* article on the subject[61] in mid-1978 suggested that the relatively poor peasantry of Trung Bo (central provinces), in contrast to their wealthier compatriots of the Mekong delta, lacked machinery and draught animals and could benefit greatly from collectivised ownership of these means of production. There was also less differentiation of plot size in the Trung Bo provinces as well as a high proportion of wasteland and communal land (land already collectively owned). The same article pointed out that commodity production (production for the market) was much further advanced in Nam Bo and that not only did the predominant strata of middle to rich peasants own their own means of production (see pp. 101–2), but they had extensive links with commerce, industry, transport and communications (which they often ran as sideline operations, primarily for profit). While the article goes on to attribute the major problems experienced in collectivising Mekong delta agriculture to factors such a lack of meticulous preparation or tight management, the implication is that the source of the difficulty lies much deeper in the type of *production relations* which had been developing in the delta zone over 30 years or more.

This assessment deserves some critical examination. It is clear from the way the argument was put in the above-mentioned article that an implicit elision was made between the development of commodity production and the rise of rural capitalism. However, while the term 'capitalist' may have applied to some Mekong delta farmers, particularly those in whose hands ownership of machinery had become concentrated,[62] it was not the case for the three-quarters of the peasantry which the regime classified as 'poor' or 'middle' peasants who in the main relied on the market to obtain means of both subsistence and production. By contrast the peasants of the central plains had remained relatively autarkic – agricultural surpluses were low and, because of the dense population, acute parcellisation of land and wartime destruction, there was a problem of how to achieve an increase in productivity which would raise peasants' involvement in the market and provoke an increased division of labour. While the Party, in 1978, saw the resistance of Mekong delta peasants as brought about by 'capitalist' influences, the real problem, as I shall argue here and in Chapter 5, was caused by the fact that many features of Vietnamese collective farms were really only appropriate to a relatively autarkic society, and indeed tended to reinforce autarky in the longer run. They could not be applied to a commodity economy without causing serious disruption.

In other words, the initial advantages of collectivisation to northern and central Vietnamese peasants lay in their ability to mobilise a plentiful off-season labour supply in an economy where both land and capital were extremely scarce. The possibilities for output increases provided by highly labour-intensive land reclamation projects, reconstruction of irrigation works, planting of windbreaks, as well as more effective distribution of means of production meant that with collective income distribution, even the wealthier peasants might gain more than they would lose in the redistribution of income and assets that the policy implied.[63] The greater mechanisation of Mekong delta farming, more abundant land and areas of labour shortage, combined with the higher development of market relations outlined in the previous section meant that such advantages were absent.

In fact the attempt to implement collectivisation in the South occurred just at a time when a vigorous debate was developing in the North on the limitations of the collectivisation so far achieved and possible ways of improving the productivity of cooperative agriculture. In the context of these discussions, the difficulties being experienced in the Mekong area brought sharply into focus the importance of labour accumulation projects (with little or no new investment in new capital equipment) in the early phases of collectivisation in the North and the subsequent difficulties in obtaining further increases in labour productivity and marketed surpluses. The experience of Vietnam's leaders up to 1976 had been based essentially on Northern conditions. The preoccupation with military matters before 1975 and the notion that their preferred model for collective rural development had scarcely been tried out, due to widespread *de facto* de-collectivisation (attributed to poor management) during much of the war period, gave them little incentive to accept the criticisms being voiced of the Northern system itself. Moreover, a high proportion of those Party members and administrators with wide *Southern* experience had been killed under the wartime Phoenix Program (which involved systematic elimination of NLF collaborators), so it is not really surprising that the depth and importance of the social and economic changes which had taken place on the ground in the Mekong delta were initially underestimated. It was some time, therefore, before the difficulties of collectivisation in the Mekong delta would lead to any new approach to the problem of agricultural production.

By mid-1978 it was clear that the economy was enveloped in a crisis, particularly in agricultural production and distribution. Real GDP growth fell below the population growth rate in 1977–8 while agricultural output fell by five per cent in 1977 and did not grow in 1978. In the South, production fell sharply in 1975 amid the chaotic conditions created by the collapse of the Saigon regime. There was some recovery in 1976 (Table 4.3), but it was not until 1980 that production surpassed its 1974 level. Average annual rice output during the last four years of the Thieu regime had been 6.7 million tonnes compared with an

Table 4.3   Paddy production by region 1975–84

Year	Whole South* 000 t	Mekong delta† 000 t	Whole country 000 t
1975	5 423.7	4 206.2	10 291.4
1976	6 640	4 686	11 866
1977	(5 987)	(4 354)	10 885.1
1978	(5 522)	(4 016)	10 040.0
1979	6 311	4 369	10 758
1980	7 307.3	5 297.8	11 678.7
1983	8 569.2	6 276.9	14 732.3
1984	9 417.6	6 931.2	15 613.4

*Provinces from Quang Nam Da Nang
southwards; †Long An, Dong Thap, An Giang,
Tien Giang, Ben Tre, Cuu Long, Hau Giang,
Kien Gian, Minh Hai. Figures in brackets are
estimates based on shares in total national
production in 1976 and 1979.
Sources   So Lieu Thong Ke, 1979, p. 59; *1930–
84,* p. 97.

estimated average of 5.9 million tonnes during the first four years of the
new one. This crisis of agricultural production threatened the Government's whole economic unification strategy not only because it
necessitated the import of large quantities of food, but because it held
back industrial recovery through lack of foreign exchange earnings, of
raw materials and of markets for industrial products.

From the point of view of the Government's aim of achieving
increased social appropriation of economic surpluses, the fall in
production in the Mekong delta during the late 1970s was accompanied
by a marked decline in State grain procurement. While it is difficult, on
the basis of the data which I have been able to unearth, to measure the
full extent of this decline, some evidence is available. *Nhan Dan* in May
1978 reported that in 1976 only 50 per cent of the state purchasing
norm for the nine provinces of the delta was met. In 1977 the rate was
'even lower' and in the first three months of 1978 (when procurement
based on the main crop of the year comes in) was 'less than half that
attained in the previous year'.[64] The article admits that the decline was
not attributable to falling production levels, but that peasants were
using their surplus paddy to raise ducks and to make alcohol. We know

that 19 per cent of the crop was collected in 1977 and from this it can be estimated that the target for 1976 must have been around 40–50 per cent in keeping with the pre-1975 marketing pattern for grain.[65] The consequences of such a dramatic drop for the Government's economic planning were clearly serious.

The strategy of bringing peasants into the collective system through State control of the trade in major agricultural products was clearly in great difficulties by mid-1978. Peasants were responding to the low State procurement prices by retreating into autarky. Falling output levels were partly due to bad weather in 1977–8, but the falls in marketed surplus were attributable to acute shortages of manufactured inputs and consumer goods which encouraged peasants either to sell produce on the free market where they could obtain better prices in order to afford high-priced manufactured goods (often State-supplied goods diverted on to the free market by corrupt officials) or to produce only enough to meet the needs of themselves and their families. Either way, production in collective fields suffered as peasants devoted maximum effort to household land.

The regime's response in mid-1978 was to intensify the efforts to create a system of 'large-scale socialist production' in the rural sector. A renewed movement was launched for the completion of agricultural collectivisation in Southern Vietnam by 1980; that is, in less than three years. Simultaneously, there was a clamp-down on the chiefly ethnic Chinese merchants, concentrated in Cholon (the Chinese quarter of Ho Chi Minh City). The aims of these measures were twofold: to achieve a large increase in agricultural output and, even more importantly, to break the system of production for the private market which was then highly concentrated, with a large number of local rice merchants locked into the commercial networks of a handful of big Cholon companies. The campaign was construed quite frankly as one of increasing the ability of the State to mobilise agricultural surpluses for its accumulation fund. Vo Chi Cong, member of the Party Political Bureau in charge of Southern agriculture, said in a speech in April 1979, that whereas tax collected on individual landholdings amounted to only 10 per cent of the harvest, with cooperativisation the percentage procured by the State could be raised to 30–40 per cent.[66] A sense of urgency was felt by Party leaders that the grain-marketing problem must be solved quickly in view of the escalating conflict with Pol Pot's Cambodia and the growing likelihood of a direct Chinese attack. The prospect of further prolonged military expenditures in a situation of reduced foreign aid availability provided the rationale and motivation for an attempt to increase sharply the rate of accumulation from domestic sources.

A full discussion of the campaign can be found elsewhere.[67] It is sufficient here to say that it was successful in driving out of business (and often out of the country) the major Mekong delta rice trading companies. Prices were also stabilised for a while. However, it did not solve the twin problems then facing the government – how to increase the total volume of agricultural production and how to siphon off the marketed surplus in such a way that not only would there be enough to meet the requirements of the urban and export sectors, but there would be greater social (as opposed to private) control over this marketed surplus. Table 4.4 shows that 1978 was the worst year of all as far as production levels were concerned and, while these began to recover during 1979, the all-important procurements by the State continued to decline. Moreover, data on State procurement of foodstuffs in the Mekong delta shows that the decline was most marked in that region. Where national procurement fell from 14 to 10 per cent between 1977 and 1979, the fall in the nine provinces of the Mekong delta was from 19 to 8 per cent. In four of those provinces, procurement fell below five per cent of output in 1979.[68]

Table 4.5 shows that in spite of strenuous efforts to open up new lands, reclaim abandoned and fallow lands and increase the intensity of cultivation, in order more fully to utilise the labour resources of the South, the area sown to paddy had increased by less than 100 000 hectares over the four year period, of which a mere 7000 hectares were in the Nam Bo region. By contrast, the north and centre of the country, with their far greater pressures of population on land, were able to

Table 4.4   Production of foodgrains and official procurement, 1975–9, 000 tonnes

	All foodgrains (paddy equivalent)	Rice	Official procurement
1975	11 591.8	10 538.9	1 690.0
1976	13 510.0	11 866.0	2 030.0
1977	12 889.8	11 885.1	1 840.0
1978	12 902.9	10 040.4	1 590.0
1979	13 727.0	10 758.4	1 402.0

Sources   *So Lieu Thong Ke 1979*, p. 55; IMF 'Socialist Republic of Vietnam – Recent Economic Developments', May 1982, p. 13.

Table 4.5   Paddy area and yields by region, 1976 and 1979

	Area sown 000 ha		Yields per crop t/ha		Share of total output %	
	1976	1979	1976	1979	1976	1979
Total	5313	5484	2.23	1.96	100.0	100.0
North Vietnam	2245	2317	2.25	1.86	42.6	40.1
South Vietnam, of which:	3068	3166	2.22	2.03	57.3	59.8
Nam Bo	2068	2075	2.27	2.10	39.5	40.6
Trung Bo*	1000	1091	2.12	1.90	17.9	19.2

*Includes all of Binh Tri Thien province, part of which lies north of the 17th parallel.
Source   *So Lieu Thong Ke 1979*, pp. 58–9.

expand their paddy area much more. The collectivisation drive in the Mekong delta certainly did not have the expected short-term effects on either output or surplus appropriation. While it is impossible to separate the actual effects from those induced by independent variables such as the weather or war damage, the official criticism of rapid collectivisation as well as the data which began to emerge in mid-1979 suggests that it was actually counter-productive.[69]

The crisis in agricultural production of 1977–80 was accompanied by declining output and availability of certain agricultural inputs and basic manufactured consumer goods. The causes of these shortages lay partly in the decline of agricultural output itself, especially in its impact on export income and the need to spend much scarce foreign exchange on food imports; partly in the increasing diversion of limited domestic and external resources to defence; partly in the coincidence of these with a number of cumulative problems in the management and planning of the economy (see Chapter 6). Of particular importance were the destruction of the North Vietnamese apatite plant by the Chinese in February 1979 and other war damage, as well as falls in coal production caused by the exodus of ethnic Chinese workers. Hence one result of the failure of agriculture, and particularly southern agriculture, to achieve a big increase in output and surplus mobilisation was to threaten a cumulative process of declining production in the economy as a whole.

THE IMPACT OF ECONOMIC REFORM

The Sixth Plenum of the Party Central Committee, meeting in August 1979, adopted new policies aimed at overcoming this economic crisis. As far as South Vietnamese agriculture was concerned, the effects of the changed direction began to be felt in 1980 following abandonment of the collectivisation drive and implementation of new marketing arrangements aimed at increasing the supply of goods by using individual incentives and the market mechanism, at the same time attempting gradually to increase the state's surplus appropriation out of the enlarged flow of goods. During 1982, following rather successful application of the system in North Vietnam, introduction of direct contracting between individual farmers and the State began. The State undertook to supply inputs in return for a grain quota at exchange rates fixed by the State. Above-quota sales could be made at a 'negotiated price' which was closer to (but normally still below) the price obtainable on the free market. Agricultural taxes and obligatory sales to the State were fixed for a five year period and were based on average yield of the contracted land over the preceding three years. One major feature of the reforms was an alteration to the price structure during late 1981, the purpose being to bring prices closer to those prevailing in the free market, to bring prices in the North closer to the higher prices in the South, and to offset the effects of a devaluation of the dong on the cost of imports. The new prices involved an increase in the official purchase price of grain, but an even larger increase in the price of manufactured inputs. This was aimed at eliminating some of the incentive to divert State-supplied inputs into the free market and to improve incentives for peasants to meet delivery quotas.

It is not easy, in assessing the results of the reforms, to quantify the effects on output of other factors such as better weather or the reduction in warfare after 1979. However, there have been substantial improvements in both output and State procurement since 1980 and the Vietnamese achieved a precarious self-sufficiency in food grains for the first time since before World War II in 1983.[70] Table 4.6 gives a summary of the situation before and after the reforms, based on the data available so far. As far as the Mekong delta is concerned, the evidence available confirms my contention that the State has greatly improved its ability to mobilise surplus grain, in spite of the apparent simultaneous flourishing of private market activity. In An Giang in 1980, for example, procurement rose to 146 092 tonnes (from 42 000 in

Table 4.6　Foodgrain production and official transactions 1975–83

	1975	1976	1977	1978	1979	1980	1981	1982	1983	1984
(1) Total foodgrain production (million t)	11.6	13.6	12.9	12.9	13.7	14.4	15.0	16.3	16.7	17.8
(2) Total domestic procurement (million t)	1.69	2.03	1.84	1.59	1.40	2.01	2.50	2.90	3.75	3.86
of which										
Agricultural tax			1.18	0.52	0.67	0.90	0.91		3.37	
Quota sales			0.66	1.06	0.69	0.86	0.86			
Negotiated sales			0	0	0.04	0.24	0.73		0.38	
(2) as a share of (1) (%)	15	15	14	12	10	14	17	17	22	22

Sources　IMF, 'Socialist Republic of Vietnam – Recent Economic Developments', May 1982, p. 13; *So Lieu Thong Ke 1979*, p. 61; *Far Eastern Economic Review*, 10 February 1983, 2 February 1984; *So Lieu Thong Ke 1930–84*, p. 159.

1977).[71] In 1983, according to various reports, Hau Giang and Kien Giang over-fulfilled their grain procurement plans and in 1984, eight out of the nine provinces of the delta met their procurement targets. In spite of this, there continued to be reports of slowness in making deliveries.[72]

Vietnamese officials do regard the improved agricultural performance of the 1980s as emanating from the new policies. However, there has been intense debate as to the longer-term role of this type of mechanism, especially in the non-agricultural sphere. Resistance to the extension of the reforms was manifested in a partial reversal taking place during 1983–5 when tax measures on private enterprise were tightened, and there was a renewed call to complete collectivisation by the end of 1985. The failure of a conservatively-inspired currency reform introduced in October 1985 appears to have shaken the government badly[73] and provided new impetus for market-style reforms. This will be discussed further in Chapter 6.

It should not be thought, however, that the extended role given to the market and slowing down of the collectivisation process necessarily represent a pulling back from the attempt to combine economic construction with the transformation of the social relations of production. The policy of collectivising agriculture in the South has continued to be a priority among all sections of the Vietnamese leadership, but this is no longer seen in the same way as before. By December 1986, the majority of Party leaders had concluded that collectivisation should be carried out *only as economic conditions allow*.[74] In other words, it is conceivable that some aspects of the agricultural labour process may never be collectivised. In any event, collective institutions are now able to take on a variety of different forms.

Thus although collectivisation of the South was indeed 'basically completed' by the end of 1985, the 'lower level' production collectives, in which some rent is paid for land and means of production contributed, tended to dominate, rather than the fully fledged cooperatives. Also there was often little difference in practice between the way these collective organisations functioned and the way 'individual' production was organised. The individual (or household) economy continued on a much larger scale than in the North, partly because of the greater availability of land, but also as a measure to retain the support of the peasantry for the collectivisation of staple food producing land. Table 4.7 gives some idea of the extent and variation of collectivisation in the Mekong delta during 1985. In addition to those shown, there are other

Table 4.7   Collectivisation in the Southern region in 1985

Province	Date	% of house-holds	% of land	Co-ops	Pro-duction collec-tives	Solid-arity teams	Other
Mekong delta							
Long An	Nov. 1985		90	23	2 664	16	
Dong Thap	May 1985	70	60		2 000		90†
An Giang	May 1985	72	77	7	2 200		
Tien Giang	June 1984	78	78				
Ben Tre	Oct. 1985	93*	91*	7–8	2 000§		
Cuu Long	Nov. 1985	73		3¶	4 106¶	30†	
Hau Giang	May 1985	71		27	6 000	2 600	48†
Kien Giang	Jan. 1986	84	79	8	3 500		
Minh Hai	Mar. 1985	70					
Eastern Nam Bo							
Ho Chi Minh	Nov. 1985	88	89	162	678		
Dong Nai	Oct. 1985	82#	82#	24	1 865		#
Song Be	Oct. 1985	85	>80	157	650		
Tay Ninh	May 1985	80	83	20	1 742		

Note   Blank spaces indicate no data found.
*Paddy land only, or about half the total cultivated area. Little attempt so far to collectivise the cash crop land.
†In Dong Thap and Hau Giang: 'inter-collectives' or federations of collectives; in Cuu Long: 'joint state-private' enterprises.
§May 1985.
¶February 1985.
#Excludes solidarity teams: a further 15% of households.
Sources   Long An: figures from Ministry of Agriculture; Dong Thap and An Giang: *SWB*, FE/1340/A/15, 29 May 1985; Tien Giang: *SWB*, FE/W1292/A/18, 20 June 1984; Ben Tre: figures from Ministry of Agriculture and from *SWB*, FE/W1339/A/21, 22 May 1985; Cuu Long: *SWB*, FE/W1341/A/18, 5 June 1985 and FE/W1330/A/24, 20 March 1985; Hau Giang, Minh Hai: *SWB*, FE/W1341/A/18, 5 June 1985; Kien Giang: *SWB*, FE/W1375/A/32, 5 February 1986; Ho Chi Minh City, Dong Nai, Song Be: respective Ministries of Agriculture; Tay Ninh: *SWB*, FE/W1341/A/18, 5 June 1985.

forms of collective organisation such as joint ventures among production collectives in Ben Tre and Dong Thap.[75]

In most cases, large means of production are held collectively, but smaller machines as well as most traditional tools and draught animals are often owned privately. In addition, according to one report, 98 per cent of Nam Bo villages had marketing cooperatives. 81 per cent had a credit cooperative,[76] established in an attempt to increase the ability of non-traditional, socially owned institutions to mobilise peasant surpluses for investment. Credit co-ops were able to offer interest rates to prospective savers of about five per cent per annum, which was higher than those offered by the state savings bank, but given the rapid inflation in the country since the reforms began, the incentive to save surplus income in this way is probably not great. Altogether, amounts recorded as being saved in State and collective institutions seem rather small.[77]

The artificiality of the earlier tendency to set 'socialisation' targets is also shown up by the 1985 collectivisation campaign. While the rate of formal collectivisation proceeded more or less according to plans laid down in Hanoi, the figures in Table 4.7 do not give an account of the real progress. In May 1985, for example, it was reported that 30 per cent of production collectives remained weak and inefficient and that some cooperatives were 'afflicted with confusion in production and business management'.[78] In Cuu Long, out of 18 cooperatives and 5337 production collectives established by the end of 1985, only half the cooperatives and less than four per cent of the collectives were regarded as being 'progressive'.[79]

During a visit to Vietnam in October–November 1985 I saw briefly a number of successful cooperatives, one production collective and a village in which production solidarity teams were, as yet, the only form of collective management (see p. 133 for definitions). I also interviewed provincial and district-level authorities in Long An, Ben Tre, Dong Nai and Ho Chi Minh City. The data collected consisted of responses to two questionnaires (one concerning district or provincial management and the other dealing with individual collectives). The aim of the questionnaires was twofold: (i) to try to find the reasons for successful performance of the collectives or cooperatives and (ii) to obtain some information on the extent of the social division of labour and the ability of the State to mobilise agricultural surpluses. Responses to the questions often suggested a further line of enquiry, according to the peculiarities of each case, and this was pursued wherever possible. Unfortunately, lack of time often prevented me from getting complete answers and from checking apparent inconsistencies in the data as reported (one scheduled morning visit to a production collective in Ben Tre had to be terminated by 8.30 because the tide went out and threatened to leave us stranded until the evening). This meant that the amount of usable data was reduced. The time factor also prevented me from obtaining historical data in some cases. Nor can the sample be regarded as in any sense representative since it is only a tiny percentage of the hundreds of cooperatives and thousands of collectives established in the South. It may, nevertheless, give a fairly good picture of the *successful* cooperatives. Nothing more ambitious could be attempted under the conditions then affecting academic research by Westerners in Vietnam. In order to put the information obtained into a wider context, however, I have, when possible, made comparisons with provincial or district averages and with results obtained by other researchers. One cooperative from the rural areas of Hanoi was also included in my itinerary.

What then can be gleaned from the responses given? In the first place, the social composition of three of the six southern cooperatives and of the production collective is different from the norm for the southern region. At Go Me cooperative, on the outskirts of Bien Hoa town in Dong Nai, at Tan Ba cooperative in Song Be, at Quyet Thang cooperative in Cu Chi district of Ho Chi Minh City and at Phu Loi Thuong production collective in Ben Tre, the vast majority of peasants were classified as 'poor' before 1975. They were either in areas controlled by the Thieu regime during the war (and therefore not subjected to NLF land reforms), or in areas heavily affected by fighting. The three cooperatives of Duong Xuan Hoi village in Long An province are the exception. Here, nine per cent of households were 'rich' or 'upper middle', 74 per cent were 'middle' and 17 per cent 'poor'. In all cases, however, private ownership of means of production and transport had been scant. The peasants in these areas could benefit, therefore, from pooling their resources and undertaking new investments through collective institutions. The one area I visited which had only gone as far as creating solidarity teams (Hung Phong village in Ben Tre) was an area of predominantly rich peasants, growing cash crops (mainly coconuts) with very little mechanisation.

The responses given suggested rather high levels of mechanisation and modern inputs (chemical fertilisers, electricity, high-yielding crop varieties) in the cooperatives – except for Tien Phong co-op in suburban Hanoi, which had mechanisation only in irrigation and relied heavily on traditional inputs. Grain output per capita ranged from 338 kg in the Ben Tre production collective to over one tonne in Go Me cooperative. These figures were all well above provincial averages, except in the case of the production collective where per capita output had nevertheless grown from a mere 69 kg per capita in 1979. High-yielding varieties were used exclusively by all the southern units studied except in one case where flooding prevented their effective use in part of the area. Other factors affecting labour productivity, such as use of chemical fertilisers, electrification and percentage of irrigated area also tended to be much higher than provincial or district averages.

As a rough indication of the degree of mechanisation in the cooperatives studied, compared with other areas of the south, I have constructed Table 4.8, comparing the number of tractors (both large and small) per hundred hectares of cultivated soil. There is insufficient data to give a more accurate representation based on the number of horsepower per hectare, but these figures do suggest that the successful cooperatives are those with mechanisation ratios at or above average for their region. It is also worth noting, in view of the argument above concerning the impact of earlier economic measures, that the ratio for An Giang province had actually fallen between 1975 and 1980. This

Table 4.8   Mechanisation ratios

Province/district/ collective	Date	Tractors/ 100 ha
Long An	1985	1.18*
Duong Xuan Hoi (3 co-ops)	1985	1.04
An Giang	1980	0.6
Cuu Long	1985	1.6
Minh Hai	1980	0.3
Dong Nai	1985	1.85
Go Me cooperative	1985	7.7
Ho Chi Minh City	1984	0.23†
Cu Chi district	1984	0.5†
Quyet Thang cooperative	1985	1.35
Tan Ba cooperative	1985	15.3
Phu Loi Thuong collective	1985	0

*State and collective only.
†State only.
Sources   Tran Thanh Phuong, *Minh Hai Dia Chi*
(Geographical Description of Minh Hai) (Ca Mau:
Nha Xuat Ban Ca Mau, 1985) pp. 95, 148; Tran
Thanh Phuong, *Nhung Trang Ve An Giang* (Pages on
An Giang) (Ho Chi Minh City: Van Nghe An Giang,
1984), pp. 96, 104; *Cuu Long Thanh Tuu 10 Nam* (Cuu
Long, 10 Years of Achievement), (Ho Chi Minh City:
Nha Xuat Ban Cuu Long, 1985), pp. 70, 88; and
results of my questionnaire.

was due to shortages of spare parts and poor maintenance which caused many machines to be cannibalised or abandoned.[80] As privately owned means of production, acquired prior to 1975, come to the end of their useful life, the concentration of these predominantly imported inputs will fall increasingly into State and collective hands – making it more difficult for farmers remaining outside the collective framework to sustain higher incomes.

The group of cooperatives and production collectives studied also appear to have succeeded in achieving above-average levels of labour mobilisation and productivity. Table 4.9 compares some indicators of these with province and district averages. In particular, the incidence of multiple cropping is higher in these cooperatives and this accounts for the greater number of labour days per annum. In the village of Hung Phong provincial authorities were concentrating on increasing labour intensity of production by introducing high yielding varieties (supplied by a series of State-owned nurseries), fertiliser, etc. Coconuts are an important resource in Ben Tre and the province has set up a number of processing factories (with help from India) and handicraft manufacturing cooperatives to stimulate local demand for output from villages like this one. But few steps had been taken to promote handicraft production of coir and twine in the villages or to establish marketing cooperatives for such products which might also have increased labour mobilisation.

Some productive diversification has taken place in most of the collectives however, the exception being Go Me cooperative where nearby Bien Hoa town provides alternative employment to farming for many family members of cooperators). Phu Loi Thuong, which is further from town than any of the others and only accessible by water, has the highest proportion of its workforce engaged in simple processing activities. In fact the proximity of the others to major market centres as well as to good communications by road and the availability of mechanised transport may be an important factor in their development. They were engaged in manufacturing such goods as lacquerware, furniture, garments (for the army), textiles and carpets for sale both on the domestic market and for export. Proximity to markets and means of transport are also important for ensuring adequate supplies of manufactured consumer goods and inputs, particularly if there are shortages or delays in State deliveries.

Some of the cooperatives also supplied information on the availability of State credit facilities. Loans were available for both long-term

Table 4.9   Indicators of labour mobilisation and productivity

Province/district/ collective	Labour-days per worker	Output per agricultural worker (t)	Cropping intensity*
Long An (1984)		1.2	1.3
An Giang (1980)			1.37
Ben Tre (1984)			1.4
Cuu Long (1984)		1.5	1.47
Minh Hai (1982)			1.05
Dong Nai (1985)	128	0.5	1.9†
Cu Chi district (1984)			1.6
Hung Phong village (1985)	100		
Phu Loi Thuong collective (1984)	180	3.4§	2.0
Go Me cooperative (1984)	250–300	2.4	2.7†
Duong Xuan Hoi (3 co-ops) (1984)		2.5	2.6
Tan Ba cooperative (1984)	218	2.2	2.6
Quyet Thang cooperative (1984)		1.2	1.7
Tien Phong cooperative (1984)			2.0†

*Total sown area of paddy/paddy area.
†Sown area of all annual crops/area of annual crops.
§1985 estimate.
Sources   *So Lieu Thong Ke 1930–1984*, p. 97; Tran Thanh Phuong, *Minh Hai Dia Chi*, pp. 38, 95; Tran Thanh Phuong, *Nhung Trang Ve An Giang*, pp. 96, 258; *Cuu Long Thanh Tuu 10 Nam*, p. 88; results of questionnaire.

and short-term production requirements, but the most interesting factor was the great variation in interest rates reported (from 3 to 36 per cent per annum and even up to 60 per cent for individual households). These differences are hard to explain without further investigation, but the high rates reported by Tien Phong (in the north) and Duong Xuan Hoi (in the south) may be indicative of efforts to increase effectiveness of investment in some areas of agriculture. This would be in keeping with a tendency to encourage more labour-absorbing methods of production and less under-utilisation of capacity than has been characteristic of cooperatives in the past. Rates for long-term loans were generally higher, on account of a scarcity of funds.

It is also noteworthy that some of the cooperatives did not complain of shortages in key areas, particularly fertiliser supplies. This is, of course, crucial to the ability to carry out multiple-cropping and mobilise surplus labour.[81] The main shortage complained about in the south was electricity. By contrast, Tien Phong cooperative suffered shortages of everything and this does seem to reflect a more general picture of the difference between North and South. This is partly the result of the more rapid expansion of export income based on agricultural products (including fisheries) and light industry in the southern region. As considerable decentralisation of the foreign trade sector has taken place under the reforms, and exporting provinces are entitled to retain a proportion of export income, the southern region has been able to expand its imports of chemical fertilisers (chiefly urea) in addition to receiving supplies of phosphate from the North. What this suggests is that, if one of the factors in the success of these cooperatives has been the higher level of modern input use, consolidation of the cooperative system will in future depend on the ability to overcome shortages of these inputs on a nationwide basis.

Other information sought related to appropriation of surpluses. As far as taxation payments are concerned, these seem rarely to have met the target of 10 per cent of output set by the State. Most sources initially said that tax payments amounted to this figure, but if pressed for details, revealed that actual payments were a smaller proportion due to yields having risen since the land was assessed. In production solidarity groups and for individual households generally, the tax rates ranged from 10 to 12 per cent.[82] Grain sales to the State in payment for State-supplied inputs ranged from 10 to 15 per cent in the case of Tien Phong (reflecting its greater reliance on traditional, non-commodity inputs) to 31 per cent at Go Me. At Hung Phong it was claimed that 70 per cent of output was sold to the State, but for cash rather than the usual barter arrangements involving exchanges of produce for inputs. While prices of commodities supplied by the centre generally did not vary from place to place, those set by provinces, districts and cooperatives varied widely.

Distribution to members was only 40 per cent of the crop in Duong Xuan Hoi, but up to 70 per cent in Tien Phong and Quyet Thang. Some of this may also be sold to the State or on the private market. In Quyet Thang deliveries to the State appear to have been quite low and the proportion of total income derived from the family economy was also higher than elsewhere.

In fact Quyet Thang had only recently received the imprimatur of 'successful' cooperative after several years of struggling to find the right formula. In 1979, the second year after its establishment, the co-op harvested 558 hectares at an average yield of 1.7 tonnes per hectare for the whole year (212 kg per head). It was criticised at the time by Vo Van Kiet (now Minister for Planning) in a speech in which he pointed to lack of adequate preparation (particularly failure to provide a warehouse and drying yard and non-completion of irrigation works)[83] or adequate draught power, fertilisers, insecticides and seeds, and for lending members of the cooperative as much as one third of its land for household use. Fifty per cent of the workers were too busy on their borrowed land to be mobilised in time for the cooperative harvest. While Kiet did not criticise the lending of land as such, he said that it had been done on too large a scale.[84] This was before the system of contracting land for produce had been sanctioned by the Vietnamese authorities.

In 1980, with the abandonment of the first collectivisation drive, many of the peasants withdrew from the co-op and only 227 hectares were harvested (at 1.3 t/ha). Things continued to get worse until 1982 when harvests on the much reduced area of 127 ha rose to 2.5 t/ha. In 1983 the contract system was introduced and the cooperative reorganised. Output in 1984 was 2.5 t/ha on 720 ha. In 1985 the co-op reported four tonnes per hectare on the first crop and was expecting a similar yield from the second crop of the year. Since 1983 the only villagers who have remained outside the co-op have been old people who, because they have no active labourers in the household are not eligible for contract land, and thus for income from the cooperative. As things stand, they are able to hire wage labour by staying outside the cooperative structure. But they do receive implements and materials from the co-op which they pay for at fixed prices.

The example of Quyet Thang appears to be a clear-cut case where the introduction of economic reforms, in particular the restructuring of individual incentives, has favoured the development of cooperative production relations. More generally, the evidence of this chapter suggests that the conditions of agricultural development in South Vietnam were such that the effort to speed up the social transformation by collectivising agriculture within the framework of an administrative planning system was at worst detrimental and at best unhelpful to the process of economic construction. Decentralisation of economic decision-making, on the other hand, by allowing an improvement in rural output, may have improved the *opportunities* for achieving an eventual socialist transformation. This would come about through increasing scope of state and collective institutions to compete effectively with the private sector and gain control of a larger share of agricultural surpluses. The importance of this lies in the enhanced ability of social (as compared with private) bodies to redistribute resources via investment and welfare decisions. The progressive retreat of the State since 1979 from direct interference in collective and household investment and production decisions and the attempt to use more economic (as opposed to administrative) levers, through provision of infrastructure and capital plus price and tax incentives should also help to overcome political opposition to 'socialism' which had arisen in response to earlier policies. Moreover, the reforms have halted a tendency to recession in the economy of Vietnam which was in turn caused by Mekong delta peasants retreating into autarky in response to acute foreign exchange (and therefore commodity) shortages exacerbated by the administered pricing system.

The operation of market forces is not itself an indication of a return to capitalism since it is the transformation of the *relations of production*, the extent of social control over the productive forces of society, which is at issue.[85] In the case of South Vietnamese agriculture however, we have seen that private control of production as well as the development of commodity relations were at a more advanced stage in 1975 than they were in North Vietnam in 1954. The problem for the post-1975 regime, therefore, has been one of how to increase the socialisation of production relations in these very different conditions without jeopardising the transition towards an advanced agro-industrial economy. The experience of the 1975–9 period showed that rapid collectivisation of land and means of production within an administrative planning framework, in emulation of most other socialist countries up to that time, was far from the best solution. The policies adopted after 1979–80 were aimed at increasing the level of socialisation of production and distribution, by creating a genuinely *national* economic system (breaking down the essential autarky of peasant household production through increasing investible surpluses, improving circulation of necessary inputs and consumer goods, creating specialised economic zones and building up district and provincial industrial complexes), but also by improving the opportunities for social control over resource allocation. Ultimately, individual farmers were to be drawn into the new collective production system by economic means rather than administrative measures.

This is certainly a very different conception of how a socialist economy should be created, from that expounded, for example, by Le Duan in 1974[86] in which he argued that collectivisation was a precondition for the construction of 'large-scale socialist production' in agriculture. The alternative position, which would appear to have gained ascendancy since 1979, is that viable forms of cooperation in agriculture cannot be consolidated without prior industrialisation and a more advanced division of labour. In southern Vietnam, while the social division of labour (in the sense of production for exchange) had developed under the former regime, the heavy dependence upon American aid led to disruption of the circulation process after the war, a disruption which was exacerbated rather than ameliorated by the transformation policies pursued by the Government. In my view, the economic crisis engendered by this combination of events highlighted the serious difficulties associated with the imposition of administrative planning on a society in which the social division of labour is already fairly advanced. The key position of the Mekong delta in the overall development strategy, was thus one of the crucial elements in bringing about a change in the conception of how to handle the socialist transformation process in the country as a whole.

5 Household and Collective in Vietnamese Agriculture

The dramatic failure of the 'Northern model' applied to southern agriculture in the late seventies brought into sharp focus the debate on the progress of collective farming in the North. Pressures for change in the 'Northern model' itself cannot be ascribed wholly to the unsuitability of collective farms for southern conditions – a number of problems had been identified even before the end of the war, while similar pressures also existed in China where outright de-collectivisation has been taking place in many areas since 1978. In fact these movements towards modifying existing collective forms in the agricultural production process echo earlier movements in the 1960s (in both China and Vietnam).

The chief problem identified in North Vietnam was low levels of labour mobilisation for collective, as opposed to household or individual, farming. Labour productivity had stagnated or declined in the Northern cooperatives in the 1970s, and with the failure of collectivisation in the South following Chinese withdrawal of commodity aid, food shortages became a serious problem; large-scale imports of rice were necessary and Vietnam's main avenue for rapidly increasing export income was lost. The need to achieve self-sufficiency in foodgrain production became an urgent necessity: it was the best way to make full use of existing productive capacity and thereby to conserve scarce foreign exchange resources. But there was a further dimension to the stagnation in North Vietnamese agriculture which was that as a result of rising population, marketed surpluses remained low. This factor will be discussed in greater detail in Chapter 7, but an indication of the size of the problem is given by the fact that in 1975, the volume of staple foodgrains delivered to the state trading network of the DRV was actually lower than in 1960.[1] While this was partly offset by expansion of trade in other crops, the level of autarky in North Vietnam's rural areas was still high. New policies were clearly needed if sustained increases in agricultural production were to be forthcoming and a genuinely national market created.

One of the major topics of debate was the role that the household as an economic unit can play in agricultural production. Until the mid-

130

1970s this discussion tended to fall within a particular rubric – household (or 'private') production was equated with 'petty commodity production' involving use of the 'law of value' and comparatively backward agricultural techniques, while collective farming was seen as part of the socialist sector amenable to modern techniques and planning. Whether or not the two sectors were seen as mutually antagonistic or complementary, the implicit assumption was that they were governed by different laws of motion and involved different social relations of production. More recently, this assumption has come into question.[2] As we saw in the last chapter, efforts have focused more on an attempt to bind farmers together through economic interdependence and this involves some redefinition of the usual conception of the 'socialised' sector.

In looking for explanations and implications of the changes, two factors need to be borne in mind: first, that the USSR, China and Vietnam have all experienced a cyclical phenomenon whereby phases of comparatively rapid progress towards collectivist forms of agriculture and tightening up of restrictions on market and household activities have been followed by phases in which there is experimentation with market-type reforms and a decentralisation of economic management. Such periods of reversion to household farming are not usually initiated as deliberate policy measures, but occur spontaneously as was the case with the growth of 'contracting' of both tasks and land in Vietnam in the early 1960s – a movement frowned upon by the authorities at the time.[3] Secondly, because of these cycles, collective and market forms of organisation in agriculture appear to many people as mutually antagonistic tendencies. Though the assumption of mutual exclusiveness is often simply asserted there is, in reality, considerable controversy over the actual theoretical relation between household and collective agricultural institutions within a socialist society.

The tightening-up phases of the cycle can be explained partly by the resistance of the socialist bureaucracy to decentralisation of economic decision-making. But they are also the result of a deeply engrained strand of socialist thought, going back to Lenin, in which the collective is the first premise of socialist agriculture. In this view collective farming is seen as the only means by which a backward agrarian society can proceed towards 'large scale socialist production in agriculture' and, more importantly from a political point of view, a mass of peasants can be transformed into an agricultural proletariat. Private or individual farming, on the other hand, is seen not only as leading to capitalism via polarisation of rural incomes – the accumulation of capital by one section of the peasant population at the same time as the poorer elements become dispossessed through indebtedness and are forced into wage labour for their better-off compatriots – but as fostering petty bourgeois aspirations among farmers who, although often poor, are nevertheless owners of their means of production and attached to market forms of exchange.

The phases of experimentation with market reforms and expansion of the role of household production, on the other hand, usually originate spontaneously at the grass roots level although, from time to time, they are also sanctioned by the authorities. While it is difficult to generalise about collective farms in a country with such widely varying conditions as Vietnam, let alone China, it does seem to be the case that the absence of certain conditions favouring collectivisation leads to pressures from below for these types of reforms. Moreover, if collectivisation is pressed in spite of this, it can lead to demoralisation of the peasantry, loss of interest in further progress towards socialism and reversion to private property (*de facto* or *de jure*) in agriculture. This is what seems to have happened extensively in China in the late 1970s and eighties, with active encouragement from a Government which possibly recognises the political and psychological consequences of years of blanket application of radical policies during the Great Leap Forward and Cultural Revolution.[4]

The aim of this chapter is to examine the conditions fostering a reversion to individual farming in North Vietnam. In Western literature it has long been argued that collective forms of agriculture are inherently doomed to failure, chiefly on account of their alleged economic inefficiency and contravention of basic laws of individualist human nature. More recently, however, there have been doubts expressed even on the Left about the viability of collective agriculture, in the light of evidence that over twenty years' experience with cooperative farming in China and Vietnam failed to produce any widespread improvements in the living standards of the peasantry or in the size of agriculture's contribution to national accumulation.

The problems of cooperatives need to be dealt with at a very concrete level, taking into account such factors as the level of development of productive forces, local climatic and soil conditions, the quality of management and technical expertise available, supplies of essential inputs and consumer goods for the peasants, the structure of the incentive system, the composition of output of different collectives and accumulation and income distribution policies. A very important consideration is the level of political consciousness of the peasantry in a given area: the extent of their involvement in revolutionary activity as well as their attachment to earlier communal institutions as opposed to market forms. At the same time, however, there do seem to be certain minimum necessary (though not sufficient) conditions for collective institutions to succeed as both social and economic units. In the absence of these basic conditions, contradictions are likely to develop resulting in the kind of cyclical movement of centralisation and decentralisation of economic decision-making noted above. If such contradictions are permitted to develop too far, then we may witness the development of political pressure for the dismantling of the collective system altogether.

HISTORICAL BACKGROUND TO THE REFORMS IN NORTH VIETNAMESE AGRICULTURE

Collectivisation of North Vietnamese agriculture was begun in 1959 shortly after the completion of a redistributive land reform. As in China, it was completed fairly rapidly; that is, in the space of two or three years, although the Vietnamese shunned many of the more radical experiments of Mao's programme and at no stage contemplated the creation of units of the size of China's communes. Following the Chinese model, Vietnam carried out collectivisation in three distinct phases corresponding to different levels of ownership of the means of production (including land). These were: (a) the creation of 'mutual aid' or 'production solidarity' teams in which land remained privately owned, but traditional forms of collective activity and tool-sharing were institutionalised, extended and put on a permanent footing; (b) formation of lower-level production collectives in which means of production were pooled and income was distributed according to labour, plus a small rent accruing to land and means of production contributed by each member; (c) advanced production cooperatives in which all land and other means of production were owned collectively and income was distributed according to work. In this phase, the common form of peasant remuneration was the work-point system.

By the mid-1960s the Party announced that collectivisation in the North was basically complete. Actually agricultural cooperativisation had been completed on paper only. Over a large part of the country a wide variety of forms of agricultural organisation continued to prevail – ranging from fairly traditional arrangements to quite advanced levels of cooperation. By that time, however, the DRV government was already heavily embroiled in fighting a war against the Americans for reunification of the country. In 1965 the United States began its Rolling Thunder campaign of bombing against North Vietnamese targets so the full attention of the Government had to be devoted to the war effort and, in particular, to keeping industrial production going. Relatively little emphasis was placed during this period on the development of agriculture, although in principle a policy designed to ensure the provision of an agricultural surplus to feed the urban population and supply raw materials to industry was followed. Industrial expansion in turn was expected to increase the supply of modern inputs for agriculture.

The reality was that the rural areas were left basically to fend for themselves. Of the little accumulation which did take place in agriculture, most went to a few select areas, especially to state farms. Foreign aid provided fertiliser, machinery and fuel. However, the main thrust of investment policy, also largely funded by foreign aid from the Soviet Union and China, was towards the industrial sector. During the war, this approach seems to have been reasonably successful in ensuring an adequate subsistence level for the rural population. Urban people, on the other hand, had to rely largely on imports of rice and other consumer goods from China.[5]

Towards the end of the Vietnam war there was a shift in the emphasis of economic policy to cope with structural dislocations caused by reduced foreign aid levels. It was unlikely that reliance on either American aid for the South or Chinese and Soviet aid for the North could be continued indefinitely.[6] Yet there would certainly be a need for investment funds on a large scale to restore the badly damaged northern industrial sector, for creating new industries to meet increased consumer demand following the ending of wartime austerity measures and for a rapid economic expansion in keeping with the socialist objective of overcoming underdevelopment. While the most important source of domestic accumulation funds was expected to be state-run industry (because of its technological advancement and high levels of labour productivity), agricultural development was also to play a role. Under peacetime conditions agriculture's increased provision of foodstuffs and raw materials to the urban sector could overcome the shortages of these goods and enable the diversion of scarce foreign exchange to other pressing needs. Achievement of grain self-sufficiency by the North would also underpin the revival of the Southern agrarian export economy while rising incomes in agriculture would stimulate the demand for industrial products and assist the growth of that sector.

If the assumption that agricultural growth would be spearheaded by the collective sector proved to be unrealistic in South Vietnam, in the case of the North itself, there were also increasing signs of stagnation in the 1970s (Table 5.1). The initial response of the Government to these problems of the rural economy was to try to reinvigorate the collectives by both improving the techniques of management and stepping up the rate of transformation of private farming (mainly in the South) and 'nominal' collectives (in the North) into advanced production cooperatives.[7] These measures prevailed from 1974 to 1979, but they were largely unsuccessful and rising political pressure from the peasantry culminated in the introduction of a series of reforms in 1979 followed by widespread adoption of product contracts in the North during 1981–2.

Table 5.1 Area, output and productivity in foodgrain production in the North, 1955–80

Year	Output 000 t	Sown area 000 ha	Yield t/ha	Labour productivity 1960 = 100
1955	4 418	2 567	1.72	
1957	4 892	2 545	1.92	
1958	5 368	2 602	2.06	
1959	6 440	2 654	2.43	
1960	5 357	2 704	1.98	100
1961	6 657	2 962	2.24	
1962	6 578	2 997	2.19	
1963	6 669	3 002	2.22	
1964	6 560	3 121	2.18	
1965–8 av.	6 726	2 945	2.28	118*
1969–71 av.	6 249	2 719	2.30	136
1972	7 071	2 755	2.57	145
1973	6 365	2 613	2.43	135
1975	5 302	2 803	1.89	130
1976	6 389	2 934	2.18	
1979	6 168	3 236	1.91	
1980	5 972	3 122	1.93	

*1965 only.

Source G. Nguyen Tien Hung, *Economic Development of Socialist Vietnam 1955–1980* (New York: Praeger, 1977) pp. 118, 127; General Statistical Office, *So Lieu Thong Ke,* Hanoi, *1979,* pp. 56–7, *1982,* pp. 56–7, *1930–84,* pp. 89–90; Andrew Vickerman, 'A Note on the Role of Industry in Vietnam's Development Strategy', *Journal of Contemporary Asia,* vol. 15 (1985) no. 2, p. 230.

The main thrust of the reforms is to achieve an incentive-driven increase in agricultural labour productivity. Where they are introduced, the new incentives replace the old work-points system of remuneration under which workers were allocated points for fulfilling task norms (measured by piece-rates or time-rates according to the type of work). The most important reform was the introduction of a system of product contracts with individual households or other small groups. Households are allocated an area of land on which to carry out certain of the more labour-intensive phases of the production process. They are allocated inputs, seeds and other services (such as mechanical ploughing) and given a target quota of grain to be supplied to the collective – a quota which is determined on the basis of productivity of the land over the previous three years. Rates at which inputs and outputs are exchanged are determined by the State, but vary from area to area according to conditions of production.

Once the contracted quota is fulfilled, the household may retain surplus grain for its own use. This can be consumed within the household, or sold on the free market or to the State at negotiated prices which are above the normal quota price, but generally slightly below the free market price. The main incentive to sell at these prices is that extra inputs can be supplied by the collective in exchange for above-quota sales. But it can also be advantageous for poor peasants who would normally have to sell their grain just after the harvest in order to pay debts and buy grain to eat in the free market at higher prices later in the year. Negotiated prices eliminate these seasonal fluctuations in price.

In many ways the contract system outlined above is similar to the 'production responsibility system' introduced in China. However, household contracting does not, as far as I am aware, involve sales of previously collectively-owned means of production to individual households, as has happened in China. Nor are households given responsibility for the entire production cycle on a particular piece of land. The jobs which are allocated to individuals under the new system are usually the most labour intensive ones, those requiring only traditional tools.[8] Mechanical ploughing, seed breeding and other technically advanced aspects of production as well as irrigation are retained by the collective and remunerated by work-points or by contracts signed with the relevant teams.[9] Welfare provision also continues to be in the collective sphere.

Individual incentives are supplemented by changes in the cooperative-level incentive system to enable collective units to retain a greater proportion of any increase in output. The main change here is that taxes and compulsory quotas are fixed for a five-year period, based on a percentage of the average output of the unit over the three years prior to the beginning of each five-year period. Increases in production during the five years are, therefore, not immediately skimmed off by the State in higher taxes and compulsory sales and may be retained for local investment and consumption needs.

There were also a series of related reforms designed to make the system more flexible and to encourage initiatives at all levels – some examples are the introduction of direct contracting between enterprises; tax holidays on land newly opened up and land reclaimed after bomb damage, defoliation or simply abandoned during the course of the war; and greater tolerance of the free market in all areas of the economy.

To what were these reforms a response? North Vietnamese collective agriculture had initially been very successful in raising output and labour productivity, mainly through expansion of the sown area due to extended irrigation works. In the early 1970s yields per hectare per crop were reported to be as high for the whole of North Vietnam as for the climatically much more favoured Mekong delta of the South – an area where private farming was predominant.[10] (However, the two areas are not strictly comparable as the northern deltas are farmed much more intensively than the Mekong delta where there is more land per labourer.) These crop yields were in themselves a significant increase over the 1950s levels. In addition, the annual land yields in the North were higher than in the Mekong delta because the expansion of irrigation under the collectives had enabled a far greater incidence of multiple cropping than could be found in southern Vietnam. The importance of these increases should not be underestimated because the population had also grown and the higher output thus reduced the quantity of grain imports needed to feed this larger population.

By the end of the 1960s these achievements had evidently run out of steam and collective agriculture was not producing the increases in output required to keep up with population growth, let alone provide surpluses for accumulation. Vietnamese analysts saw the problems as falling into two categories: those relating to declining labour productivity and labour mobilisation in the collective sector and those relating to the increasing importance of individual households in both production and distribution of output.

The problems were acknowledged to be widespread. In fact it would appear, from Fforde's study in particular, that not more than five or ten per cent of collectives could be regarded as successful or 'model' cooperatives; that is, those achieving high performance figures with successful organisation along cooperative lines. At least 70 per cent of cooperatives fell into the 'nominal' category – namely, those organised only on paper according to the guidelines laid down by the State. Therefore, it must be said that it is difficult to ascertain how much the cooperative framework had contributed to output growth at all, given that the statutes were clearly not applied in a large number of places.

An article in the historical journal *Nghien Cuu Lich Su* in 1977, for example, stated that 'the situation of cooperators taking over collective land without permission ... is generalised and has been so for many years'.[11] Moreover, 'almost all' cooperatives were failing to operate according to the rules for establishing work norms and income distribution according to labour.[12] A paper at the 1974 Thai Binh Agricultural Conference implied that in the majority of cooperatives 'the cooperative avoids performing certain tasks and gives them to the families of cooperators.'[13] Other cooperatives handed out 'blank contracts' to teams and brigades so that the so-called 'plan' of the cooperative was in practice determined purely by the wishes of the relevant units.[14] A survey carried out in 1972 found misappropriation of funds on a 'massive scale'.[15]

On the question of labour productivity in the collective sector, it was pointed out that the time required to produce a given quantity of paddy had been rising instead of falling.[16] Thus while peasants were nominally putting in more days per year, the productivity of their labour had not increased and had even begun to decline. This meant that production levels were, in the main, unable to rise much above subsistence requirements and even renewed the spectre of famine which had haunted the North during the colonial period. Worse still, the collectives seemed unable to increase the rate of labour mobilisation. One analysis stated that the average number of days members worked for their cooperatives was only 200 per annum while the average length of the working day was a mere five to six hours.[17] (*Nhan Dan*, in June 1978, gave an alternative estimate of only four to five hours.[18]) In five 'model' cooperatives studied by Adam Fforde, the percentage of available labour force actually used in the cooperatives ranged from as low as 62 per cent up to 92 per cent.[19] What happened in the 'nominal' cooperatives is not known. A related question here is the amount of actual effort put in by those who did turn up for collective work. It has often been suggested, in relation to collective farming, that inadequate incentives have led to low intensity of work and this has been confirmed for Vietnam.[20]

The *Nhan Dan* article previously cited related the issue of labour mobilisation and productivity to that of privatisation in arguing that the decisive factor in declining crop yields in the collective sector was not bad weather (as in contemporary official pronouncements for overseas consumption), but the concentration of manpower in the household plots (the so-called 'five per cent land'). The survival and expansion of household farming, which was then generally equated with backwardness and retardation of socialist development in Vietnamese writing, was thought to be occurring at the expense of labour mobilisation and improved productivity in the collective sector.

In what follows we will examine more closely the reasons for the stagnation in rural productivity in order to re-appraise this apparently antagonistic relationship between the collective and household sectors in agriculture. This will give a better idea of the sorts of cooperative arrangements which could become feasible in both North and South in the future.

LABOUR MOBILISATION AND LABOUR PRODUCTIVITY

What lies behind the low turnout of labour on most collective farms simultaneously with the high level of attention to family plots? The answer to this question should lead a good part of the way towards an explanation of why, in approximately 70 per cent of cooperatives, insufficient surplus has been available in the past for accumulation and modernisation and why the social division of labour has failed to develop rapidly in the northern half of the country.

Two main problem areas can be identified in relation to this question: the first lies in the very concept of 'large-scale socialist production in agriculture'; the second lies in the structure of incentives (both collective and individual) which operated in Vietnam from the inception of cooperative farming.

1. Large-scale socialist production

Until the late 1970s, the socialist governments of both China and Vietnam persistently ignored, in practice though not always in theory, Lenin's warning that large-scale collective farming could not be consolidated without industrialisation, that is, the widespread use of modern inputs and mechanisation. Lenin had been insistent in his writings on the nature of large-scale agriculture, especially in his various commentaries on Kautsky's *Die Agrarfrage*, that large-scale did not mean simply farms covering a large area of land or employing large numbers of labourers. Looking at Germany, he contrasted the large Prussian *junker* farms which were really feudal estates using backward methods of production and were gradually being broken up under the impact of capitalist development, with the sometimes tiny, but very efficient because highly capitalised, farms of the new capitalist farmers.[21] For Lenin, then, the crucial features of 'large-scale agriculture' were the economies of scale which could be derived from utilising modern technology.[22]

Prior to the late 1970s, however, the Vietnamese seem to have been closer to the Chinese conception, spelled out by Mao Zedong, that changes in the social relations of production could *themselves* force an advance in the forces of production.[23] It was alleged that in spite of a lack of industrial inputs, the forces of production could be increased by using labour accumulation (irrigation works, for example), an increased division of labour and product specialisation with concentration of certain crops in geographically suitable localities.

These factors, especially the new division of labour in the cooperatives (in which workers were divided into specialised teams for soil preparation, irrigation, cultivation, etc.), gave them a veneer of industrialisation where in fact none (or at best very little) existed. However, this division of labour was not analogous to an industrial division of labour at all because it was based on traditional technology and did not lead to economies of scale. The labour intensive techniques of rubber tapping or rice transplanting, for example, are such that it is *technically* no more efficient to have ten labourers working a farm of 100 hectares than for the same ten labourers to be working on their own small plots of ten hectares each. It is not intended to deny altogether the possibility of productivity gains from the reorganisation of labour into teams or brigades by cooperatives, but it does suggest that the new division of labour was imposed often without any real basis for expectation of such improvements and, when combined with other elements affecting productivity of labour, may have had a negative effect (see discussion of individual incentives, page 150).

These observations are lent credence if we also consider that a major difference between most modern industrial production and agricultural production (whatever the level of productive forces), is that factory work is in its essence cooperative: each individual in the production line is incapable of producing final output without the cooperation of the other workers in the factory. The technologically determined division of labour ensures that production itself is fully *socialised*. In agriculture, by contrast, production is sequential, taking place over a lengthy period of the year and farmers, even those using quite sophisticated techniques in many cases, are able to carry out the tasks on their own. Cooperation is not an essential aspect of the labour process, except in tasks like harvesting, pest control and irrigation which have, in any case, traditionally been carried out by joint effort in Vietnamese villages. Note, however, that even in these activities, cooperative labour is unlike factory labour in the sense that it is non-specialised.

It is also important to remember that even in the most advanced capitalist countries, many aspects of the labour process do not correspond to Marx's category of Modern Industry. Farmers, for example, although often using the most up to date technology (computers, lasers, etc.) are normally involved in a highly individual labour process. Where a division of labour exists within the enterprise (in an Australian shearing shed, for example), it has more in common with the earlier divisions Marx categorised as Manufacture than with the machine-dominated division of Modern Industry. The different type of division of labour in capitalist agriculture is independent of the institutional framework – the private ownership of the means of production by individual farmers – which can be seen on plantations (the nearest to factory production of all agricultural enterprises) but is related to the peculiar characteristics of agriculture mentioned above. Similar points can be made about the labour process in other important sectors of advanced capitalism – transport, commerce, the civil service. This widespread existence of a non-industrial type of division of labour in even the most advanced capitalist nations has largely been ignored within the socialist literature. From Lenin onwards, socialists have aimed to make the labour process in agriculture as technically similar as possible to the labour process of modern capitalist industry.

Capitalist farmers do, however, live in an environment in which production is highly socialised, unlike the relatively autonomous peasant households of older agricultural systems. They depend upon the productive activities of others in order to carry out their labour process, but in this case, the socialisation of production is mediated through the system of exchange; it does not take place directly within the labour process of the enterprise. If the development of modern industrial systems is to be seen, as I suggested in the introduction to this book, in terms of the progressive development of the division of labour and generalisation of exchange, it is all the more important in dealing with an economy like that of Northern Vietnam, in which relative autarky and traditional techniques prevail, to focus on the social division of labour as the basis for economic growth.

According to this view of the technological characteristics of Vietnamese agriculture, the creation of specialised soil preparation, cultivation and irrigation teams in the absence of any change in the methods of production was a rather artificial practice. In the words of a Vietnamese author, Le Thu Y,

> the degree of production integration and specialisation is low, and cooperation and division of labour within cooperatives as well as between cooperatives and the national economy is neither comprehensive nor far reaching. Operation of this collective production body demands a certain necessary coordination among organs and elements, but it has not reached the point of synchronisation such as found in the operation of a completely mechanised agricultural enterprise. . . . *The peasant has not yet been bound firmly to collective production by an economic power such that apart from the collective he could not exist.*[24] [Emphasis added]

What collectivisation did produce in Vietnam was a once and for all increase in output during the 1960s. This is because the labour accumulation projects, particularly the widespread construction of irrigation schemes, enabled the virtual doubling of output per hectare by increasing cropping intensity. Under private agriculture systems, disputes can arise over irrigation if it is left up to individual farmers to maintain the channels and dykes or if water allocation is not centrally organised (recent travellers to China have reported an increase in such disputes following the break-up of communes). The existence of a permanent, collective responsibility for irrigation works is an important factor in ensuring the continued ability of all farmers in a locality to achieve multiple cropping. However, the existence of a collective (or even state) responsibility for irrigation does not necessitate collective *cultivation* – as is shown by the experience of 'nominal' collectives in the DRV.

It seems likely that the reported increases in output of North Vietnamese agriculture in the early 1960s (before the American bombing commenced) can be largely attributed to the once-off effects of these labour accumulation projects under the auspices of the collective units.

The increases enabled the people of the densely populated Red River delta, especially, to shift away from the brink of starvation which had been a persistent threat during the colonial period. At the same time the early successes, combined with the fact that the war effort took most of the attention of the Vietnamese leadership during the late 1960s and early seventies, probably were responsible for blinding the leadership to the fact that while yields per crop had risen somewhat, labour productivity remained low and, moreover, diminishing marginal product of labour had set in. In any case, it was not until a significant decline in both yields and labour productivity occurred in the mid-1970s and debate ensued, that there was recognition of the failure of the new division of labour to bring about substantial economies of scale.

The first point, then, about the traditional conception in socialist theory, at least as interpreted in East Asia, of progress towards 'large scale socialist agriculture' is that there was an artificial imposition of a division of labour, not based on any technological imperative, from which it was assumed that industrialisation of the agricultural forces of production would ensue. The increases in yields which did come about after collectivisation were not, however, due to this division of labour (except where it was justified by introduction of new methods in a minority of cooperatives), but to the once and for all effects of capital accumulation via labour-intensive projects – especially in irrigation. Other gains from the reorganisation of labour may well have taken place, but these are likely to be specific to certain crops and/or geographical zones.

2. Incentives

Whether or not the division of labour in agriculture can ever become strictly comparable to the classic industrial case, it clearly is not so in Vietnam or countries like it today. A major problem arising from this has been to devise an appropriate system of incentives, at both the levels of the collective and of individual cooperative members, which will draw the agricultural population into a more advanced division of labour.

(a) Collective Incentives These will be dealt with here under three main headings: (i) the system of surplus appropriation and investment; (ii) the determination of output mix and related pricing questions; (iii) the social objectives of the cooperatives. These are all areas in which the

macroeconomic and social goals of the State may come into conflict with the immediate interest of cooperative management, perhaps leading to disincentive effects for the cooperative as a whole.

(i) Firstly, there is the possibility of excess savings-rates arising from the pressure of higher-level authorities for unrealistically high levels of planned investment. Nolan[25] argues that, given the predominantly self-financing nature of the Chinese communes, a policy-induced over-emphasis on accumulation led to peasant dissatisfaction with the rate of growth in their standard of living. High accumulation rates out of collective income tended to restrict the growth of individual incomes. To support his argument here, he points especially to the case of wealthy suburban communes with large numbers of tractors, etc., which were inefficiently utilised – often standing idle or in a state of disrepair. This is a case, he suggests, where strong disincentives to extra effort on the part of commune members are present: they know that any increased income which results will be absorbed in further accumulation (or go to the State in taxation) without leading to a rise in their own living standards.

While this is undoubtedly a description of the situation in a small minority of very wealthy communes on the outskirts of Shanghai or Canton (prior to the reforms), it may also be apposite for cooperatives at the other end of the income scale. Many Vietnamese cooperatives, for example, which were not strictly speaking producing a surplus to subsistence requirements, were still expected to meet taxation and quota sales to the State plus accumulation-fund shares, and consequently had little left over for internal distribution, while receiving scant investment from the State itself. In such cases, the demands of the State would tend to discourage peasants from devoting extra time and energy to cooperative production.[26]

However, the picture is not a simple one and bears closer examination. According to one prominent school of thought,[27] if investment rates are high and the consumption share of income is compressed, it is true that after a certain period, as the new capacity created by the investment comes on stream, consumption levels can nevertheless begin to rise rapidly and will eventually reach much higher levels than would have been possible with an initially higher consumption share. Indeed if the consumption share is too high and fails to make adequate provision for replacement of worn-out equipment, etc., it is possible for standards of living to fall.

This kind of analysis has been criticised for its over-simplification of the problem, and needs to be modified in some important ways for the Chinese and Vietnamese cases. As I have pointed out in Chapter 3, if we are dealing with an economy in which direct producers are living at or close to a (socially defined) subsistence minimum, compression of the share of consumption in order to raise the rate of investment can have a zero or negative effect on the rate of growth unless rising productivity allows an increase in living standards at the same time. A major concern of planners then, is to ensure that capital-output ratios are not increased to the point where declining or stagnant per capita consumption puts a brake on labour productivity.

Significant increases in living standards become possible as a result of completion of labour accumulation projects, that is, creation of new capital stock which is not financed out of the accumulation fund of the collective. But when diminishing returns to labour accumulation projects set in, the failure to provide sufficient funds (either from the cooperative or from individual households) for investment will lead to stagnating and even declining income distribution from the collective and to pressure for greater access to the free market.

One possibility of achieving improved capital–output ratios is based on the theoretical contributions of writers like Kalecki and Lowe.[28] The former pointed out that an absolutely essential component of the growth process is the *effectiveness* with which increases in the capital stock are utilised. The latter pointed to the importance of achieving the correct balance between different sectors of the economy through investment policy – particularly the correct proportions between investment in industries (or agriculture) producing means of production to build producer goods, those producing means of production to manufacture consumer goods and those producing consumer goods. Such concern with proportionality was, of course, an essential part of Marx's writing on expanded reproduction (in Volume II of *Capital*) and of numerous writers who have taken his reproduction schemes as a starting point. Modern input–output models, working at much lower levels of aggregation than the earlier versions, owe their origins to this theoretical insight.[29] Unless investment decisions take into account existing input–output relations in the economy, then it is impossible for increments to the stock of means of production to be utilised effectively and, however high the share of investment in national income, the rate of growth actually achieved will be low.

The type of investment undertaken is therefore crucial. But this is by no means the only important component of investment effectiveness:

management policies, individual incentive structures and the organisation of labour will also contribute to the effectiveness of new capital stock and these are important determinants of the rate at which technical innovations are embodied in it. Unless these factors are also taken into account, the full impact of any given investment package will not be felt.

In China, when the incomes of peasants and workers were finally raised in the late 1970s this might have led to a sudden unsustainable increase in imports or to inflation and/or queuing (which would have wiped out the incentive effect of the higher money incomes) if there had not already been a substantial amount of industrial growth based on the investment of the past 25 years. (Note, however, that if this investment had been used more effectively, such income increases could have occurred earlier and consumption might by now have been even higher). In the case of Vietnam, this is exactly what has happened. The very considerable investment effort of the 1960s was heavily damaged by the combined effects of American bombing in 1965-8 and 1972 and the Chinese invasion of North Vietnam in 1979.[30] The difficulties of planning to achieve the proportionalities required to ensure the most effective use of new capital stock under the conditions of risk and uncertainty brought about by war and the changing allegiances of erstwhile aid donors are obvious. The Vietnamese leadership probably paid insufficient attention to the problem in any case: its preference was for concentrating efforts in the heavy industrial sector. The little industry which had been established in the south of the country was heavily dependent on supplies of imported raw materials, as indeed was the Southern agricultural sector, and most of the consumer goods available to the Southern population were also imported. The consequences of the increases in consumer demand which followed the end of the war in the North and again after the reforms of 1979, were simultaneous upsurges in the import bill, in black marketing of smuggled consumer items, in inflation and queuing – all consequences of acute shortages brought about by lack of an adequate industrial structure.

Vietnamese industry has, prior to 1975, suffered from severe disproportionalities, and in 1982 average capacity utilisation was still only 45-50 per cent.[31] In agriculture, crucial areas of shortages are in the supply of electricity, chemical fertilisers, fuel, consumer goods and transport facilities. Thus no matter what microeconomic reforms might be introduced into the collective farming system, they could not by themselves alleviate the lack of incentive at the enterprise level, caused by ineffective investment patterns in the economy as a whole.

It would seem, then, that the problem is not simply one of a choice between high and low rates of investment, since, depending on the circumstances, either policy can have counter-productive effects on peasant commitment to collective forms of ownership and production organisation. A low rate of investment can lead to a low growth rate of the economy or, if the new capacity created is used efficiently, it can lead to an improved growth rate and ultimately to much increased consumption levels than will a much higher rate of investment where capital is used ineffectively and individual incentives are wiped out by transgression against the consumption constraint. With a given rate of investment, however, the problem is most importantly one of composition of investment, especially the division between investment in industries producing machinery to build machines and machines to produce means of production for consumer goods. Moreover, within these categories, attention must be paid to the composition of investment between producer goods for industry and agriculture.

What determines the composition of investment in a socialist system is a question we shall leave to the next chapter. The importance of this point, however, is shown by the fact that in China, the introduction of the production responsibility system was accompanied in many instances by improved supplies of high quality seed and fertiliser, better availability and type of storage facilities, making it difficult to attribute the higher incomes obtained to the new incentives on their own.[32] The Vietnamese leadership has been critical of its own policy of neglecting investment in industries producing modern inputs for the farm sector.[33] What this has meant is that cooperatives faced with shortages have resorted to the black market[34] or to privatised methods of obtaining necessary inputs and even then, these may be insufficient.

(ii) The question of excessive interference in the assortment plan of industrial enterprises is a well-known source of disincentive in socialist economies: there may also be a similar problem with agricultural units, of centrally imposed plan targets which affect composition of output. Grain policy has been cited as a possible cause of dissatisfaction with cooperatives, and Nolan[35] argues that the policy of imposing self-sufficiency on the Chinese communes committed them to concentrating a large amount of effort in the production of a crop for which remuneration – at the low state procurement price prevailing – was rather poor compared with the possibilities offered by high-priced industrial or secondary food crops. This policy of encouraging each cooperative to be self-sufficient in grain also operated (and still does, but at the district or provincial level rather than the cooperative) in Vietnam. It is hard to see what other sort of policy could have been followed by the Vietnamese Government, for a number of reasons. Firstly, grain self-sufficiency would be the spontaneous response of the majority of cooperatives in any case since it was the traditional cropping pattern in the country. The traditional pattern is reinforced by the lack of a developed national market or adequate transport network to enable different localities to concentrate on production of crops more suited to their natural conditions or fetching a better market price than rice.[36] Moreover, such adjustments in the traditional cropping pattern would require careful investigation of soil and climatic conditions as well as economic factors: most cooperatives lacked the technical expertise to carry out such inquiries on their own.

No substantial adjustment to the traditional pattern of local rice self-sufficiency could be made, therefore, without the intervention of the State. But, before 1975 at least, the Vietnamese State was almost wholly preoccupied with the war effort and could devote little attention to investment in the infrastructure to support agricultural development. For the most part, a policy which, apart from injections of Chinese-supplied consumer goods, amounted to benign neglect, resulted in an adequate supply of basic foodstuffs in the rural areas and the Government could rely on cheap and sufficient imports of grain from China to feed the urban population. With the cessation of this aid from China after the war, the concentration of efforts on expanding grain production domestically became even more imperative, especially given the rapid rate of population growth (officially estimated at about 2.7 per cent), so there was little likelihood that in the short-term there could be a relaxation of the existing grain policy. The alternative would have been an expensive crash program of infrastructure building plus high intermediate levels of grain imports – both using scarce foreign exchange reserves.

A corollary to this argument is that changes in the price structure of agricultural crops would have had little effect on the predominant cropping pattern. On the other hand, an increase in the procurement price for rice relative to industrial goods could have been an important incentive for peasants to work more effectively in the cooperative fields. Low procurement prices were one means by which the State planned to transfer surplus out of agriculture by reducing urban wages costs, but increased labour productivity of cooperative rice production obtainable with a higher price might also enable a larger surplus to be extracted without squeezing peasant incomes. At the same time, an increased supply of rice could be expected to have a depressing effect on the open market price, helping to eliminate parallel markets and, in the long run reducing the need for subsidies from the State budget on urban food prices.

Official data show that in fact agriculture's terms of trade (in official prices) tended to improve prior to the late 1970s,[37] particularly the terms of trade for grain. However, these improvements were apparently insufficient to offset rising costs of production caused by low labour productivity and shortages of inputs leading to low capacity utilisation and unprofitability of grain production.[38] Since the 1979 reforms, the official terms of trade have worsened as prices of State-supplied inputs were raised more sharply than grain procurement prices.[39] But given that farms previously had to rely much more on the open market for inputs (at higher prices) or suffer shortages, increased availability of lower-priced State goods may mean an effective improvement in the terms of trade of individual farms (without adversely affecting the cost structure of State-run industry). Thus provided the improvement in State-supplied inputs can be sustained; the prospects of better profitability of grain production can become a reality.

(iii) The third area in which collective incentives may be important in determining labour mobilisation and productivity in cooperative farming is that of income distribution. Much of the discussion more properly belongs under the heading of individual incentives (discussed on page 150), but it has been suggested,[40] again in the case of China, that the collective provision of welfare has led to excess egalitarianism and may have prevented the proper functioning of income distribution according to work. If the cooperative does try to guarantee a minimum subsistence for its members (working or otherwise) and provide certain other basic facilities such as schools and clinics, there is a danger in a poor enterprise that very little income will be left over for distribution on the basis of the workpoint system – thus the existence of the welfare system may in itself lead to disincentive effects, as well as leading to a shortage of accumulation funds. This is an argument which strikes at the very heart of the cooperative system. The ability to guarantee a subsistence minimum to disadvantaged members and to improve the social consumption of all, is precisely one of the main reasons for the establishment of collective institutions in the first place. A distinction needs to be drawn, however, between the distribution of income within the cooperative and the *level* of income of the cooperative as a whole.

Judgements need to be made as to whether the relief of absolute poverty would be better achieved by the use of individual incentives in which income more accurately reflects effort expended to raise the overall living standard of the co-op members, or by continued provision of a welfare fund. The implications of abolishing welfare funds for the poorest and most disadvantaged sections of the population will depend very much on the effect of the economic reforms on overall output levels and the extent to which the State is able to provide emergency relief.

One of the chief conclusions to be drawn from this discussion is that policies which work for one part of the country do not necessarily work for all areas. High rates of accumulation may be possible and successful in one area while others may need considerable State assistance (not always possible under given macroeconomic conditions) before they can begin to approach the ideal of advanced socialist agriculture. But even more important is that there is no clear coincidence of interests of individual cooperatives with the objectives of the State, or even (in the case of welfare, for example) with those of different cooperative members. A policy of maximising income distribution to members may conflict with overall industrialisation policy, result in inflation or excessive import bills in the short term and eventually prove counterproductive due to lack of investment. On the other hand, high rates of accumulation, especially if investment is not carefully balanced between sectors can clearly lead to poor productivity of farm workers and severely limit the overall *level* of investment. In the same way, movement in the real terms of trade against agriculture can affect adversely the Government's ability to extract a surplus from the rural sector. Yet what increases the productivity of cooperative farm labour in the short run does not necessarily lead to the highest growth rate in the longer run. These are problems which cannot be solved theoretically, but require practical experimentation and flexibility of policy to take into account differing conditions from one part of the country to another.

(b) Individual Incentives   While it is bound to be difficult (if not impossible) to find a system of collective incentives which satisfies both the criteria of economic efficiency (in the microeconomic sense of orthodox economics) and the macroeconomic and social objectives of the State, problems have also arisen in designing a suitable array of individual incentives for cooperatives. Thus, while the workpoint

system of income distribution was intended to allocate collective income according to work contributed (indeed some authors[41] have erroneously referred to it as a 'piece-rate' system), in actuality income has not always been closely related to work done. The difficulties of quality control in many agricultural tasks resulted in the introduction of time-rates for many jobs, and another problem arose from the allocation of workpoints according to tasks completed (so many hectares ploughed, weeded, etc.), though these were only partly related to final output. Those charged with delivering manure, for example, may be tempted to dump it at the edge of the field, leaving it to others to spread it properly, without affecting the number of workpoints they earn. Similarly, there is little incentive for careful soil preparation if yields may still be poor due to inadequate supplies of fertiliser or late transplanting. The problem is that final output, under these circumstances, is not the responsibility of any particular team or individual and there is a strong incentive to maximise the number of workpoints earned by, say, ploughing a large area too shallow, in the hope of obtaining a larger share of an indeterminate crop. Moreover, the rather narrow range within which workpoints were distributed may give rise to a disincentive effect since income will not always reflect variations in energy expenditure of different individuals.

Many of these difficulties arise from the peculiar nature of the division of labour in agriculture. In particular, supervision of the labour force has proved to be an important obstacle to the efficient use of a big workforce on large farms. Abhijit Sen,[42] has pointed to the difficulties (in the Indian context) of the supervision of wage labour in agriculture caused by spatial dispersion and the need for farm workers to use both judgement and timing in carrying out many cultivation tasks. If there is a tight crop schedule, as is the case in the double- and triple-cropped areas of Vietnam, the question of correct timing of operations becomes very important. Sen builds up a convincing case that where traditional methods are used, private capitalist farmers will find it unprofitable to hire more labour than they and their families are able to supervise closely. Farmers owning large areas of land will tend to use alternatives to wage labour, such as sharecropping, as a means of avoiding supervision problems – this is because productivity of wage labour tends to fall in cases where it cannot be closely watched. Sharecropping, by contrast, not only offers the labourer greater incentives by tying income to effort expended, but by thus improving the productivity of the labourer it also increases the overall profitability of the enterprise to the landowner when compared with the profitability of an equivalent farm area cultivated by wage labour using the traditional techniques.[43]

According to Sen's analysis, however, it is possible for the capitalist farmer to increase his returns even further where he can use mechanisation to raise the productivity of a relatively small labour force. While hypothetically the same result can be achieved with a large number of labourers using oxen or buffalo as with one labourer using a tractor, the preferred solution of the farm owner will be for the more mechanised technique because it effectively eliminates problems of labour supervision. Mechanisation is also superior to sharecropping (with traditional techniques) in this respect because, Sen found, there are disincentive effects in the latter case stemming from the fact that the labourer does not receive the full benefit of his increased effort, but has to hand over a fixed proportion to the landowner. But mechanisation is not simply a choice of technique: it involves a shift to a new technological environment in so far as a certain industrial capacity (to provide spare parts, fertilisers, etc.) and the existence of adequate repair facilities and infrastructure are required. That is, a certain level of the development of the productive forces is a pre-condition for 'large-scale agriculture' in the sense that use of industrial technology leads to increasing returns to scale.[44] Moreover, large-scale agriculture is more efficient, according to Sen, *only* when there are no problems of a supervision constraint.

This analysis can be applied to collective farms in a socialist economy as well as to capitalist farms. The technical similarities are clear: northern and central Vietnamese agriculture is characterised by the use of traditional techniques, plentiful supply of labour and lack of a technological environment favouring immediate mechanisation of most farms. The incentive structure which existed before 1979 (in law if not in actual practice) was one which, like the wage system in capitalist agriculture, did not relate income of individual cooperators directly to effort expended. The workpoint system therefore incorporated some disincentive effects relative to the incentives to work in household plots where remuneration was closely related to work. Moreover, the parts of Sen's analysis which concern the problems of supervising a large, spatially dispersed workforce apply also in the case of Vietnamese cooperatives, particularly given the shortage of experienced and highly skilled management personnel. There is an additional problem in the case of collective units which is that, owing to difficulties with the *collective level* incentives outlined above, there may be lack of interest by brigade and/or cooperative management in supervising work closely. Such a difficulty does not arise in the case of the capitalist farm. But leaving this possibility aside, it is clear that problems of labour productivity under the system of collective organisation before 1979–80, could be substantially ascribed to the 'supervision constraint' (meaning that with traditional techniques, the most effective alternative to tight supervision and control of the labour force on large farms is a system of incentives which relate remuneration to work, in such a way that supervision becomes unnecessary).

On collective farms where mechanisation *has* taken place, the problem of supervision should be less pressing than on a capitalist farm where the entire surplus is appropriated by the employer. Evidence from China supports this view: Gonzalez[45] found that opposition to the production responsibility (although superficially of an ideological nature) tended to come from communes with higher mechanisation and lower dependence on agriculture as the principal source of income. Provided the system of individual and collective incentives is organised in such a way that farmers can experience both rising real incomes over time, and remuneration at least partly in proportion to effort expended, to the extent that this happens, supervision may be less necessary.

HOUSEHOLD AND COLLECTIVE AGRICULTURE IN VIETNAM

In much of the academic discussion, debate about the use of market reforms, however limited these may be, revolves around the question of the relationship between household and collective agriculture.[46] These concerns go back to worries about Lenin's New Economic Policy in the Soviet Union of the 1920s and the possibility that it would lead, via increasing differentiation in the countryside, to the establishment of a strong rural capitalist class. The implicit assumption in much writing on the subject is that the development of individual or family-based farming occurs at the expense of socialisation and is an obstacle to it. In this view, family plots and the use of the law of value in price determination in socialist societies are relics of old modes of production.[47] While it is not denied that they are necessary features of the early phases of the transition to socialism, there is an assumption that they will wither away as part of the process. In fact there is very little evidence to support such a view in any of the socialist countries – even in the longest established of them, the Soviet Union, family plots are not only persisting, but generally have the highest yield in Soviet farming; and this is true even of the most advanced agricultural regions.[48] This high productivity of private plots also applies to Vietnam.[49]

Experience suggests, moreover, that efforts to tighten up on household activities by using 'administrative methods' are often counterproductive.[50] Considerable evidence has emerged from both Vietnam and China in recent years that efforts to persuade peasants to devote less attention to their five-per cent plots (the five per cent of collective land allocated for household use) and more to the collective crops not only failed significantly to raise the mobilisation of labour in the collective fields, but tended to drive the household activities underground (namely the illegal occupation of land). Moreover, this kind of repression of household activity carries with it the overtones of forced collectivisation – something which has been explicitly rejected by Vietnamese leaders from earliest times. In a situation of acute and chronic shortages of all types of goods ranging from necessary productive inputs to consumer goods, such a system also puts great power in the hands of managers and cadres who are in a position to dispose of resources. This can lead to favouritism based on kinship or political ties.[51]

An alternative view is that household and collective farming are complementary in some way. At a purely descriptive level, it is well known that in Vietnam the collective provides the basic subsistence food of the population, rice, while the individual plots are the main source of secondary food crops like vegetables and of livestock, particularly pigs.[52] The Vietnamese author, Nguyen Huu Dong, has referred to the possibility of using family plots as a means of mobilising extra labour. He suggests that it is only by using the five-per cent plots to encourage peasants to work for three or four hours over and above the normal eight-hour day contributed to the cooperative, that the full labour resources of the economy become available.[53] Another view which sees interdependence between collective and household sectors is that put forward by Karl-Eugen Wadekin, writing on the USSR. He bases his conclusions on a reading of the Soviet literature on the subject and argues that the collective sector has been in fact very dependent upon the health of the 'private' sector and would not have been able to survive in its absence without running into acute political and social problems. However, Wadekin's study also implies that as the socially defined level of subsistence in the Soviet Union has risen with the higher productivity of the agricultural sector as a whole, the proportion of labour-time devoted to family plots has fallen and productivity and incomes in the collective sector have risen (chiefly due to mechanisation).

While the dependence of the collectives on the household sector is fairly well established by Wadekin, something he did not examine very closely is the reverse type of dependence. One such case, pointed out by Christine White, is that of peasants in North Vietnam taking in grain from the collective for drying in their own yards on a contract basis. White argues that before collectivisation, absence of local brick and tile manufacturing made household drying-yards scarce. The collective is unable to dry all its grain without such sub-contracting because of a lack of space for such a large quantity. So the very creation of collectives has provided the initial stimulus for and now sustains an important area of household activity.[54] Other possible examples of this type of interdependence are the use of mechanised ploughing done by the collective sector which, by saving ploughing time, releases labour for cultivation of household plots. The existence of certain welfare aspects of cooperatives is another factor which might enable household economic activity to expand its scope: child care facilities, for example, can free the women of the collective to devote more time to family plots. White also points out that the nature of family-plot farming is changed fundamentally under the collective system by the fact that it is no longer possible for the household to go bankrupt and lose its land.

It is clear then, that there is considerable interdependence between the two sectors of household and collective agriculture, but to analyse the system of social relations governing these interdependencies it is necessary to look at the mode of surplus appropriation.

The case against expansion of household-based farming in countries like Vietnam rests on the assumption that it leads to increasing private appropriation of the social surplus – that peasants, while depending upon the collective to provide basic subsistence, will use cash incomes from household land to accumulate capital. There is an implicit equation, in this argument, of goods exchanged in the free market with the existence of a *surplus* which is available for accumulation. But this is not the case in North Vietnam because the income derived from marketing household produce is used in order to meet family consumption needs (manufactured goods such as pots and pans, bicycles, textiles or foodstuffs not produced locally).[55] The size of the family plots on all collective farms in the North is so miniscule that they could never provide a surplus sufficient for the accumulation of major means of production. And since there is no market in land, families cannot accumulate capital in this way either. Moreover, the areas where illegal land occupation did occur tended to be those where the struggle to achieve a minimum subsistence living was precisely the most intense (but see p. 157 for the case where household surpluses do arise).

An alternative theoretical position on the relationship between household and collective farming can be based on the analogy with the role of subsistence agriculture in capitalist economic systems. The function of subsistence agriculture under capitalism is to provide basic consumer items to the wage labour force, thus reducing the overall cost of production to the capitalist by enabling him to pay lower wages. Continued existence of petty agriculture (garden plots) is often encouraged by employers as a means both of keeping wages in the capitalist sector below socially defined, or even physical, subsistence levels and of tying the workforce to a given locality and ensuring a plentiful supply of labourers willing to turn up for low wages. This is an important phenomenon in plantation agriculture where this method of ensuring a cheap labour force has obviated the need for mechanisation in areas like tea-picking and rubber-tapping.

On collective farms where methods of production are still largely labour-intensive and cooperative fields are, as yet, unable to supply enough means of subsistence to satisfy the needs of the population, the analogy also applies. In both cases, the income from the agricultural enterprise (capitalist farm or collective farm) is divided into two parts – that which goes towards the consumption needs of the producers and that which is a surplus and goes towards investment and accumulation (or tax). In both cases the subsistence plot provides additional income to the workers enabling the enterprise to lower the share of its income which must be devoted to maintenance and reproduction of the workforce. While the collective fields provide the most important part of peasants' subsistence requirement, it is unlikely that such subsistence plots will disappear when living standards begin to rise. On the assumption that basic subsistence requirements can be met in future from an increasingly mechanised cooperative sector, the household plots will concentrate more and more, as in the Soviet Union, on higher quality and more expensive items of consumption. However, it is also likely that as peasant income from the collective crops and industries rises with mechanisation, the more backbreaking labour of the family plot will become a less urgent priority.

The analysis can be taken a step further by focusing on the economic surplus. In the collective system the investible surpluses are concentrated in the socialised sector rather than the household plots. In many